# FOCUS ON SUCCESS

The new edition
Ausgabe Technik

## Vocabulary Practice Book

Elizabeth Hine

Cornelsen

**Focus on Success – The new edition: Ausgabe Technik** wurde geplant und entwickelt von der Redaktion Moderne Fremdsprachen des Cornelsen Verlags, Berlin.

| | |
|---|---|
| Verfasserin: | Elizabeth Hine, Berlin |
| Projektleitung: | Jim Austin |
| Verlagsredaktion: | Kari-ann Seamark |
| Redaktionelle Mitarbeit: | Fritz Preuss |
| Layout und technische Umsetzung: | Kathrin Eitdorf, Berlin |
| Umschlaggestaltung: | werkstatt für gebrauchsgrafik, Berlin |
| Titelfotos: | Alamy RF/R. Broadwell, Alamy/A.Kowalsky, Fotofinder/Visum/A.Krug, GettyRF/Datacraft |

**Erhältlich sind auch:**

| | |
|---|---|
| Schülerbuch | ISBN 978-3-06-020228-7 |
| Workbook | ISBN 978-3-06-020270-6 |
| Handreichungen für den Unterricht mit CD-ROM und Audio-CDs | ISBN 978-3-06-020273-7 |

**www.cornelsen.de**

1. Auflage, 1. Druck 2009

Alle Drucke dieser Auflage sind inhaltlich unverändert und können im Unterricht nebeneinander verwendet werden.



Druck: CS-Druck CornelsenStürtz, Berlin

ISBN 978-3-06-020282-9

Inhalt gedruckt auf säurefreiem Papier aus nachhaltiger Forstwirtschaft.

# Inhaltsverzeichnis


## Refresher course

| | | |
|---|---|---|
| Unit A | Free-time activities | 4 |
| Unit B | Girls fight for their rights | 6 |
| Unit C | You are what you eat | 8 |
| Unit D | Time out | 10 |
| Unit E | Shopping | 12 |
| Unit F | Ready for a job? | 14 |

## Main course

| | | |
|---|---|---|
| Unit 1 | City lights | 16 |
| Unit 2 | Advertising | 20 |
| Unit 3 | Media madness | 24 |
| Extra vocabulary | Advertising & media | 28 |
| Unit 4 | On the move | 30 |
| Unit 5 | Green enough? | 34 |
| Extra vocabulary | Transport & environment | 38 |
| Unit 6 | Modern ways to work | 40 |
| Unit 7 | Going global | 44 |
| Unit 8 | Finding a job in the EU | 48 |
| Extra vocabulary | Work & globalization | 52 |
| Unit 9 | Social challenges | 54 |
| Unit 10 | Multiculturalism | 58 |
| Unit 11 | Crime | 62 |
| Unit 12 | Future life, future living | 66 |

## Technical Topics

| | | |
|---|---|---|
| Topic 1 | Internal combustion engines | 70 |
| Topic 2 | Electricity | 72 |
| Topic 3 | Tools | 74 |
| Topic 4 | Materials and their properties | 76 |
| Topic 5 | Energy | 78 |
| Topic 6 | Safety | 80 |
| Topic 7 | Supplying the global market | 82 |
| Topic 8 | Technical jobs | 84 |
| Topic 9 | Low-energy building technology | 86 |
| Topic 10 | Easing the load | 88 |
| Topic 11 | Data collection and storage | 90 |
| Topic 12 | Robotics | 92 |

## Answer key 94


**Abbreviations and symbols**

| | |
|---|---|
| *AE* | American English |
| *BE* | British English |
| *abbrev* | abbreviation |
| *n* | noun |
| *v* | verb |
| *adj* | adjective |
| *inf* | informal |
| *phr* | phrase |
| <> | opposite |

# A Free-time activities

| | | |
|---|---|---|
| **ability** | skill | Fähigkeit |
| **according to** | as reported by | nach, gemäß |
| **to be lucky** | not: ~~to have luck~~ | Glück haben |
| **to chill out** | *(inf)* to relax | sich entspannen |
| **currently** | at the moment | zurzeit |
| **to discover** | *n* discovery | entdecken |
| **employer** | *v* to employ | Unternehmer, Arbeitgeber |
| **to expect** | *phr* to expect sb to do sth | erwarten |
| **to get a lot out of sth** | to benefit from sth | viel davon haben |
| **to go clubbing** | to go out to clubs, to go dancing | in Discos gehen |
| **to hang out** | to spend a lot of time in a place | rumhängen |
| **instead of** | rather than | statt, anstatt (von) |
| **to manage** | to control sth, to deal with sth | zurechtkommen, fertig werden (mit), (es) schaffen |
| **mate** | *(inf)* friend | Kumpel |
| **movies** | *(AE) BE:* cinema | Kino |
| **net** | *(abbrev)* internet | Internet |
| **to network** | to connect computers | vernetzen |
| **ordinary** | normal | gewöhnlich, normal |
| **part-time job** | *v* to work part-time | Teilzeitarbeit |
| **permanent** | <> temporary | ständig, dauerhaft |
| **pub** | *(AE) BE:* bar | Kneipe |
| **qualification** | *phr* job qualifications | Qualifikation, Ausbildung |
| **to refer to** | to talk about sth specific | sich beziehen auf |
| **skill** | thing you are good at | Fähigkeit, Geschick |
| **suitable** | appropriate | passend, geeignet |
| **to surf** | *phr* to surf the net | surfen |
| **survey** | set of questions used to find out people's opinions | Umfrage |
| **valuable** | useful, important | wertvoll |
| **voluntary** | *v* to volunteer | freiwillig (tun) |
| **worthwhile** | important, worth doing | der Mühe wert |

**Replace the underlined words with suitable words or phrases from the vocabulary list on page 4. You might need to rephrase some of the sentences.**

1 Neil <u>works</u> in a clothes shop <u>a few days a week</u>.

______________________________________________

2 We usually go <u>clubbing</u> in the city centre.

______________________________________________

3 I like <u>relaxing</u> on the beach on holiday.

______________________________________________

4 Kerstin and Danni are my best <u>mates</u>.

______________________________________________

5 I spent a year doing <u>unpaid charity</u> work in India. It was hard but <u>worth doing</u>.

______________________________________________

6 Scientists haven't <u>found</u> a cure for cancer yet.

______________________________________________

**2** **Now find your answers in the wordsearch.**

| | | | | | | | | | | | | | | |
|---|---|---|---|---|---|---|---|---|---|---|---|---|---|---|
| A | P | R | I | T | Y | B | Z | C | E | Q | K | A | L | P |
| U | A | X | D | I | S | C | O | V | E | R | E | D | V | J |
| W | R | F | G | R | Y | N | P | A | B | Q | G | K | I | F |
| L | T | D | N | H | X | O | M | U | P | Z | A | W | V | R |
| K | T | G | E | D | A | N | C | I | N | G | Y | O | L | I |
| R | I | N | T | E | Y | Q | Z | P | W | E | R | R | T | E |
| N | M | B | W | V | C | X | Y | L | K | J | U | T | G | N |
| A | E | S | O | F | H | K | Q | E | R | T | P | H | L | D |
| Q | J | C | R | S | R | G | N | J | I | L | P | W | M | S |
| P | O | L | K | M | J | Z | G | C | D | E | Q | H | Y | A |
| L | B | J | H | I | Z | R | E | T | Y | M | A | I | H | U |
| I | G | V | O | L | U | N | T | A | R | Y | Z | L | O | S |
| T | T | A | F | H | K | P | I | Z | R | W | Q | E | A | D |
| C | H | I | L | L | I | N | G | O | U | T | G | J | K | M |
| B | C | G | O | T | O | T | H | E | P | U | B | O | P | A |

# B Girls fight for their rights

| | | |
|---|---|---|
| **at least** | at the minimum | mindestens |
| **to back off** | to stop making things difficult for sb | zurücktreten |
| **to ban** | to say that sth is not allowed | verbieten |
| **to beat** | to win against sb | schlagen |
| **to compete** | to play against other people or teams | konkurrieren |
| **to disappoint** | *adj* disappointed | enttäuschen |
| **equal** | person who is treated the same as others | Gleichberechtigte/r, Ebenbürtige/r |
| **to forbid** | *adj* forbidden | verbieten |
| **frightening** | scary | erschreckend |
| **impression** | a feeling or idea about sth | Eindruck |
| **to injure** | to hurt sb | verletzen |
| **joke** | *phr* to tell a joke | Witz, Scherz |
| **loser** | <> winner | Verlierer/in |
| **muscle** | tissue that moves a part of the body | Muskel |
| **nasty** | not nice | gemein |
| **next door** | in the next room or building | nebenan |
| **opponent** | person or team who plays against sb | Gegner/in |
| **proud** | to be pleased with oneself | stolz |
| **requirement** | thing that is necessary | Erfordernis |
| **shiver** | *phr* a shiver of fear | Zittern |
| **statement** | *v* to state | Aussage |
| **stretcher** | piece of equipment used to carry sb who has been hurt | Trage |
| **teammate** | person who is on the same team as you | Mannschaftskamerad/in |
| **to teach sb a lesson** | to show sb they were wrong by making sth bad happen to them | eine Lektion erteilen |
| **to twist** | to turn | (ver)drehen |
| **tough** | difficult, strict | zäh, streng |

## 1 What do the underlined words and phrases mean? Choose the correct definition.

1 Petra lives next door to me.

☐ a Petra's room is the next room you will come to.
☐ b Her house and my house are next to each other.
☐ c She is a very good friend of mine.

2 Her aggressive behaviour isn't helping. I told her to back off and ignore him.

☐ a She should stop causing more problems and not talk to him.
☐ b She should stand a few steps away from him when he gets aggressive.
☐ c When he comes into the room, she should turn her back and pretend he isn't there.

3 I was so nervous at the interview. I hope I left a good impression.

☐ a I spilled my coffee at the interview. I hope I didn't leave a mark on the table.
☐ b I hope they remember how nervous I was at the interview. Then they'll know I really want the job.
☐ c I hope they remember me in a positive way.

4 Last season Lakeside School beat us at volleyball.

☐ a Pupils from Lakeside School were very aggressive and hit us at the last game.
☐ b The Lakeside School volleyball team won the game against us.
☐ c We won the volleyball game against Lakeside School.

## 2 Match the words that mean the opposite. There are two extra words you don't need. What are they and what do they mean in German?

proud — tough — joke — opponent — nasty — loser — teammate — disappointed — winner — nice — easy — compete

______________________ ______________________

______________________ ______________________

# C You are what you eat

| | | |
|---|---|---|
| **addiction** | *v* to be addicted | Sucht |
| **ashamed** | *n* shame | beschämt |
| **attitude** | *phr* attitude towards sth | Haltung, Einstellung |
| **cheeky** | rude but in a funny way | frech, kess |
| **community** | people who live together in an area / a society | Gemeinde |
| **curable** | *v* to cure | heilbar |
| **to disagree (with)** | <> to agree with | widersprechen, nicht zustimmen |
| **eating disorder** | e.g. anorexia, bulimia | Essstörung |
| **embarrassed** | *n* embarrassment | verlegen |
| **evidence** | proof | Beweis, Beleg |
| **familiar** | *n* familiarity | bekannt |
| **genuine** | real | echt |
| **to get drunk** | to drink so much alcohol that you can not think clearly | sich betrinken |
| **to have room** | to have enough space for | Platz haben |
| **in no time** | very quickly | im Handumdrehen |
| **to lose control over** | to no longer be able to control sth | die Beherrschung verlieren |
| **to overcome** | to beat or deal with (a problem or illness) | überwinden |
| **to pull oneself together** | to take control of your feelings | sich zusammenreißen |
| **to put on weight** | <> to lose weight | zunehmen |
| **to refuse** | to reject, to turn down | ablehnen |
| **research** | study to find out more about a subject | Forschung |
| **secret** | *phr* to keep sth secret | geheim |
| **sympathetic** | *n* sympathy | mitfühlend, verständnisvoll |
| **task** | work, assignment | Aussage |
| **time off** | *phr* to take time off | Freizeit |
| **to throw up** | to be sick | (sich) erbrechen |
| **treatment** | e.g. medical treatment | Behandlung |

## 1 Read the text and work out the anagrams.

Everybody at work liked Chris - he was a friendly guy with a KEECHY[1] smile. Then one day his life changed: his mother died and his girlfriend left him. He started drinking alcohol to make himself feel better. He kept missing days at the office and finally lost his job. Soon he was drinking early in the morning and didn't TEG RUNKD[2], even after drinking large amounts of alcohol. He stopped eating properly and lost a lot of GEIWHT[3]. He felt that he could no longer control his drinking. His friends were worried and asked him if he had a problem, but he was too embarrassed and DRUFESE[4] to talk to them.

One day, he decided to tell his family about the problem. They were PATSMITCHEY[5] and got medical TAERTTENM[6] for him. At first it was really difficult but he met people at the centre who had experienced the same problems as him. He slowly began to put on weight and have a more positive DUTETAIT[7] towards life. It took a long time, but Chris has managed to MORCOEVE[8] his alcohol problem. He is looking for a new job and I'm sure he will find one in no time!

1 ________________

2 ________________

3 ________________

4 ________________

5 ________________

6 ________________

7 ________________

8 ________________

## 2 Read the text again and find words which mean the same as the words below.

1 lost control ________________

2 ashamed ________________

3 get fatter ________________

4 very quickly ________________

# D Time out

| | | |
|---|---|---|
| **absolutely** | definitely | absolut |
| **to break into** | to enter by force | einbrechen |
| **bright idea** | clever idea | glänzende Idee |
| **come on** | used to show that you think sb is wrong | komm (schon) |
| **comfortable** | pleasantly relaxed | bequem |
| **definitely** | certainly | bestimmt, definitiv |
| **destination** | place to which people travel | (Fahrt-)Ziel |
| **especially** | particularly | besonders |
| **exotic** | exciting because it is strange or unusual | exotisch |
| **farewell** | goodbye | Abschied |
| **financial** | *v* to finance | finanziell |
| **flight** | journey made by plane | Flug |
| **to give sb a lift** | to pick someone up and take them somewhere | mit dem Auto mitnehmen |
| **living expenses** | money spent on basic things | Lebenshaltungskosten |
| **to pick fruit** | to take fruit from trees or plants | Obst pflücken |
| **proper** | real | richtig, geeignet |
| **school-leaver** | person who has just left school | Schulabgänger/in |
| **several** | a few more than one | mehrere, einige |
| **time out** | *phr* to take time out | Freizeit |
| **to take off** | (of a plane) to leave the ground | starten |
| **visa** | stamp in a passport which allows you to enter a country | Visum |
| **to watch out** | to be careful | aufpassen |
| **weatherman** | person on TV who predicts the weather | Meteorologe |

**1** **Read the dialogue. Find eight mistakes and correct them.**

| | |
|---|---|
| **Tim** | Do you know what you're going to do when you leave school? Are you going to look for a job or take some time up? |
| **Michelle** | I want a <u>real</u>[1] job. I really need to earn some money! And you? |
| **Tim** | I'm getting my visum for Australia later. I'm going to work on a farm for 6 months. |
| **Michelle** | You'd better be <u>careful</u>[2], I've heard there are lots of dangerous snakes in Australia. What are you going to do on the farm? |
| **Tim** | Help with the animals, pick fruit, help in the kitchen, things like that. |
| **Michelle** | You? Help in the kitchen? But your cooking is really awful. |
| **Tim** | I'm sure I can learn. You can give me some suggestions. |
| **Michelle** | OK. And what do you want to do after your 6 months on the farm? |
| **Tim** | Travel in Asia. After 6 months I should have enough money to cover my live expenses. |
| **Michelle** | Wow! I wish I was going to such <u>exotic places</u>[3]! But how are you going to pay for your fly? It's really expensive to fly to Australia. |
| **Tim** | Well ... My grandparents are paying for it. It's my $18^{th}$ birthday present. |
| **Michelle** | Lucky you. Now I wish I was going somewhere exciting, but I just don't have enough money. How could I earn £1000 so quickly? Any dark ideas? |
| **Tim** | Well, you could break out of the school at night and steal all the computers ... |
| **Michelle** | Come in, Tim! Are you going to the school lefters <u>goodbye</u>[4] party on Saturday? |
| **Tim** | Yes, do you want me to <u>pick you up</u>[5]? The party starts at 9, so I could come at 8.30. |
| **Michelle** | OK, good idea. Thanks. |

**2** **Read the text again and find synonyms for the <u>underlined</u> words or phrases.**

1 ______________________

2 ______________________

3 ______________________

4 ______________________

5 ______________________

# E Shopping

| | | |
|---|---|---|
| **assistant** | person who assists sb | Verkäufer/in |
| **bargain** | special offer | Sonderangebot |
| **to buy sth on credit** | to buy sth using borrowed money | etw auf Kredit kaufen |
| **convenient** | *n* convenience | bequem |
| **department store** | large shop selling clothes, food, etc. | Kauf-, Warenhaus |
| **fabulous** | great, wonderful | fabelhaft |
| **fashion-conscious** | very interested in fashionable clothes | modebewusst |
| **feature** | aspect of a product | Eigenschaft |
| **honest** | *n* honesty | ehrlich |
| **irresponsible** | <> responsible | unverantwortlich |
| **to keep in touch with** | to stay in contact with | in Verbindung bleiben |
| **mail-order catalogue** | book of products which you can order by phone or post | Versandhauskatalog |
| **obviously** | clearly | offensichtlich |
| **occasional** | now and then, sometimes | gelegentlich |
| **purchase** | *v* to purchase | (Ein-) Kauf |
| **pushy** | aggressively trying to persuade sb to do sth | aufdringlich |
| **reliable** | which can be trusted | zuverlässig |
| **to repay** | *n* repayment | zurückzahlen |
| **retailer** | person or company that sells products | Einzelhändler/in |
| **to run up debts** | to spend more money than you have | sich verschulden, Schulden anhäufen |
| **sale** | event where goods are sold at a cheaper price | Schlussverkauf |
| **shoplifter** | person who steals things from a shop | Ladendieb/in |
| **shopping trolley** | shopping cart | Einkaufswagen |
| **staff** | *phr* a member of staff | Personal, Mitarbeiter |
| **thrill** | *adj* thrilling | Spannung |

**1** **Complete the sentences with the English equivalent of the German word in brackets.**

1 She borrowed a lot of money from different people. I hope she can pay her ____________ (*Schulden*).

2 The staff in there are really ____________ (*aufdringlich*), they never let you look around the shop in peace.

3 Good luck in your new job! And keep in ____________ (*Verbindung*)!

4 We have to ____________ (*zurückzahlen*) the bank at a rate of 19% per year.

5 That new software has got lots of great new ____________ (*Eigenschaften*).

6 I hear they are looking for new ____________ (*Mitarbeiter*) at the airport.

7 I bought lots of cheap clothes in the ____________ (*Schlussverkauf*) this morning.

8 There aren't any more ____________ (*Wagen*). We'll have to carry our shopping to the till.

**2** **Decide which word is the odd one out and say why.**

1 staff - shoplifter - department store - customer

____________

2 irresponsible - fabulous - thrilling - honest

____________

3 bargain - sale - 2 for 1 - debt

____________

4 mail-order catalogue - credit - online shop - supermarket

____________

# F Ready for a job?

| | | |
|---|---|---|
| **at a disadvantage** | having more problems than other people | benachteiligt |
| **careers adviser** | professional who gives people advice about jobs | Berufsberater/in |
| **careless** | <> careful | sorglos |
| **cashier** | shop assistant | Kassierer/in |
| **to complain about** | *n* complaint | reklamieren |
| **to concentrate** | to focus on sth | sich konzentrieren |
| **day off** | *phr* to take a day off | freier Tag |
| **to deal with** | to work with | sich beschäftigen mit |
| **to depend on** | to be influenced by | abhängen von |
| **don't mention it** | you're welcome | gern geschehen |
| **to fit** | to be suitable | passen |
| **to get by** | to have just enough money to live | durchkommen |
| **to hand in** | to give in | abgeben |
| **job-related** | e.g. job-related skills | beruflich |
| **loads of** | a lot | eine Menge |
| **misunderstanding** | *v* to misunderstand | Missverständnis |
| **nowadays** | these days | heutzutage |
| **objection to** | *v* to object to | Ablehnung |
| **part-timer** | person who works part-time | Teilzeitarbeiter/in |
| **questionnaire** | list of questions | Fragebogen |
| **recently** | lately, not long ago | kürzlich, neulich |
| **sensible** | <> silly | vernünftig |
| **to sit back** | to relax and not play an active role in sth | sich zurückhalten, sich zurücklehnen |
| **social life** | time spent meeting friends | Sozialkontakte |
| **to stay up** | to not go to bed | aufbleiben |
| **to take it in turns** | to alternate | sich abwechseln |
| **to text** | to write a text message | SMS schicken, simsen |
| **tuition** | *v* to tutor | Unterricht |

## 1 Look at the list on page 14 and match the verbs and prepositions. There are two prepositions you don't need.

| | | | |
|---|---|---|---|
| 1 | hand | a | on |
| 2 | deal | b | under |
| 3 | get | c | with |
| 4 | stay | d | by |
| 5 | depend | e | at |
| 6 | sit | f | up |
| 7 | complain | g | about |
| 8 | object | h | back |
| | | k | to |
| | | l | in |

## 2 Fill in the gaps with one of the phrasal verbs from above.

**1**

**Kelly** I've got so much homework to do. I'll have to ______________________ late to finish it all.

**Mum** ...

**Kelly** Oh Mum!

**2**

**Rachel** Yesterday I ____________________ to the restaurant manager ____________________ the service.

**Mandy** Why?

**Rachel** ...

**3**

**Jo** Did Becky manage to ______________________ that difficult customer?

**Alan** ...

## 3 Match the correct dialogue parts from the list below.

A I don't know. She's gone home now. I'll send her a text and ask her.

B The waitress was so careless. She brought us the wrong food three times and didn't even say sorry!

C If you spent more time on your homework and less time on your social life, you wouldn't have this problem.

# 1 City lights

| | | |
|---|---|---|
| **amazing** | impressive | erstaunlich |
| **to be stuck** | to be unable to get away | feststecken |
| **calm** | quiet | ruhig |
| **to check out** | to find out about | herausfinden |
| **to contrast** | to compare differences | gegenüberstellen |
| **downtown** | *(AE) BE:* city centre | im Stadtzentrum |
| **elevator** | *(AE) BE:* lift | Aufzug |
| **to feature** | to appear | eine Rolle spielen |
| **to get used to** | to become familiar with sth | sich gewöhnen an |
| **I guess** | I suppose | ich glaube |
| **huge** | very big | gewaltig |
| **never-ending** | non-stop | unaufhörlich |
| **nightmare** | *adj* nightmarish | Albtraum |
| **non-stop** | never stopping | non-stop |
| **particularly** | specific, especially | bestimmt, speziell, besonders |
| **presenter** | *v* to present | Moderator/in |
| **quotation** | *v* to quote | Zitat |
| **to scan** | to read sth quickly | überfliegen, absuchen |
| **really something** | something impressive | etwas Besonderes |
| **to receive** | to get | empfangen |
| **roughly** | <> exactly | ungefähr |
| **rural** | <> urban | ländlich |
| **shopping mall** | *(AE) BE:* shopping centre | Einkaufszentrum |
| **skyline** | buildings etc. that can be seen against the background of the sky | Silhouette |
| **skyscraper** | very tall building | Wolkenkratzer |
| **suggestion** | recommendation | Vorschlag |
| **traffic** | cars/buses etc. on the road | Verkehr |
| **urban** | <> rural | städtisch |
| **to yell** | to shout | schreien |

## 1 Put these words in order according to size.

village metropolis city town

++ ____________

\+ ____________

\- ____________

\- - ____________

## 2 Find the words which mean the opposite (3 pairs) and those which mean the same thing (4 pairs).

shout huge endless calm urban tiny downtown non-stop amazing city centre yell rural stressful impressive

| Opposite | | The same | |
|---|---|---|---|
| | | | |
| | | | |
| | | | |
| | | | |

## 3 Read the sentences. Cross out any options which are not possible.

1 I'll be home late tonight. I'm stuck in cars / traffic / the lift.

2 At first, she found life in the country boring, but now she can't imagine living anywhere else / has got used to it / wants to move back to the city.

3 The traffic here is non-stop / very calm / a nightmare.

4 Check out that skyscraper – it's huge / endless / amazing!

5 I guess / think / believe Sandy will want to visit the big malls downtown.

# 1 City lights

| | | |
|---|---|---|
| **borough** | part of a city which has its own local government | (Stadt-)Bezirk |
| **characteristic** | quality | Eigenschaft, Merkmal |
| **crowded** | filled with people | überfüllt |
| **cultural** | connected with culture | kulturell |
| **to differ** | to be different | sich unterscheiden |
| **to draw** | to attract | anziehen |
| **effect** | result | Auswirkung |
| **ethnic** | connected with origin/race | ethnisch |
| **every ... under the sun** | all possible kinds of | jedes ... unter der Sonne |
| **to explore** | to travel around and see different areas | erkunden |
| **immigrant** | *n* immigration | Einwanderer/in |
| **including** | *(abbrev)* incl. | einschließlich, inbegriffen |
| **to invent** | *n* invention | erfinden |
| **large-scale** | in large numbers | in großer Zahl |
| **man-made** | <> natural | von Menschenhand |
| **melting pot** | place where people from different cultures live together | Schmelztiegel |
| **population** | the number of people living in an area | Bevölkerung, Einwohner |
| **sense** | a feeling | Sinn, Gefühl |
| **to strengthen** | to make stronger | stärken |
| **structure** | something that has been built | Gebäude |
| **to take sb's breath away** | to surprise sb by being very impressive | jdm den Atem rauben |
| **taxpayer** | person who pays taxes | Steuerzahler/in |
| **unemployment** | *adj* unemployed | Arbeitslosigkeit |
| **variety** | *adj* various | Vielfalt |

**1** **Read the text and work out the anagrams.**

Dear Diary

This is my seventh day in Dellview, North Carolina - the smallest town in the USA! No, sorry I think New Amsterdam in Indiana is smaller. Only one person lives there! Dellview has an official PLPUIANOTO[1] of approximately ten people. It has recently experienced a wave of MIMIGATROIN[2] from New York though - Mom, Dad, Richie and I! Dellview is not really a cultural TMENGLI TOP[3] like New York. Only four families live here ...

The nearest "metropolis" to Dellview is Cherryville where I will go to Cherryville High School in September. In New York I always took the WORDECD[4] subway to school. Here a school bus will pick me up every day. Mom and I are going to PLOREEX[5] Cherryville tomorrow and watch a movie in the evening. The movie theater there WDRAS[6] many people from the surrounding towns and villages - there is of course no movie theater in Dellview!

Why did Dad have to get a job in North Carolina? I really miss Queens, the borough where we lived in the Big Apple. It is so different from Dellview! There was a real RIETAVY[7] of nationalities in our neighbourhood - Chinese, Italian, Latin American, in fact you could probably find every culture and nationality DERNU HET UNS[8]!

Our apartment on the 22$^{nd}$ floor had a great view over the New York skyline - on a sunny day it really took your RABETH[9] away. Dad says that he loves living out in the country, away from all those NAM-DAME[10] structures and where it is so quiet at night. But I miss the sound of people talking and hanging out on our street and the cars driving past. You really got a NESES[11] of living in a city that never sleeps.

Today I found out that people in Dellview don't pay tax! Mom said that is because there is only one road in the town and no hospital, fire service or school. But why should other YATPAXESR[12] pay for our small road! When I am old enough, I want to move back to New York. Maybe Richie will come with me.

# Advertising

| | | |
|---|---|---|
| **advertisement** | *(abbrev)* ad, advert | Anzeige, Werbespot |
| **agency** | e.g. advertising agency | Agentur |
| **aim** | goal | Ziel |
| **annoying** | irritating | lästig, ärgerlich |
| **banner ad** | advert that covers the top/ bottom of an internet page | Bannerwerbung |
| **to be due to** | to be because of | darauf zurückzuführen sein |
| **brand** | *phr* brand name | Marke |
| **campaign** | *phr* advertising campaign | (Werbe-)Feldzug, Kampagne |
| **classified** | arranged by subject | nach Rubriken geordnet |
| **client** | customer | Kunde/Kundin |
| **commercial** | advertisement | Anzeige, Werbespot |
| **to decline** | to decrease | abnehmen, sinken |
| **to design** | to create | entwerfen |
| **developer** | person whose job is to create new products | Entwickler/in |
| **freelance** | e.g. freelance journalist | freiberuflich |
| **to get the green light** | to be allowed to begin | grünes Licht erhalten |
| **to launch** | to start | einführen, starten |
| **leaflet** | flyer | Broschüre, Flugblatt |
| **PA** | *(abbrev)* personal assistant | persönliche/r Assistent/in |
| **pop-up ad** | advert that appears on the screen when you are online | Internet-Anzeige |
| **product placement** | advertising products by showing them in films / on TV | Schleichwerbung |
| **to promote** | to advertise | fördern |
| **to set up** | to start | begründen |
| **shortlisted** | chosen to go on a list of possible candidates | in der engeren Wahl |
| **slot** | appointment | Termin |
| **sponsorship** | giving financial support to a group/event etc. | finanzielle Unterstützung |

**1** **Find eight different kinds of advertising in the word search below.**

| | | | | | | | | | | | | | | | |
|---|---|---|---|---|---|---|---|---|---|---|---|---|---|---|---|
| A | Q | Q | I | E | F | L | Y | E | R | L | O | S | I | P | A |
| P | I | Z | R | W | A | D | G | H | K | Y | S | C | B | R | N |
| M | B | C | Y | S | F | H | K | P | I | T | P | R | W | O | A |
| B | P | E | I | U | Z | T | R | E | W | Q | O | A | K | D | L |
| A | L | P | O | P | U | P | K | J | H | G | N | F | D | U | S |
| N | A | M | N | B | V | C | X | Y | A | A | S | D | F | C | G |
| N | H | J | K | L | E | Q | E | R | W | R | O | T | Z | T | U |
| E | I | O | P | L | M | K | O | I | J | N | R | B | H | P | U |
| R | Z | G | V | C | F | T | R | D | X | S | S | E | W | L | A |
| Y | A | P | O | S | T | E | R | Z | I | L | H | Y | R | A | J |
| M | K | E | R | O | D | N | A | S | Y | N | I | E | Q | C | N |
| C | L | A | S | S | I | F | I | E | D | L | P | A | B | E | F |
| K | E | I | F | Z | L | O | H | A | E | S | B | T | R | M | L |
| R | M | P | G | D | J | F | K | X | S | T | N | R | D | E | U |
| T | V | C | O | M | M | E | R | C | I | A | L | C | H | N | K |
| P | E | H | F | F | E | K | O | D | F | Z | I | S | V | T | R |

**2** **Complete the sentences with the missing word endings below. There are two endings you don't need.**

-ting -er -tion

-listed -lance -ment -ship

1 His latest novel has been short ______________ for the Booker Prize.

2 Annabel is a free ______________ web designer.

3 Our company wants to win sponsor ______________ of the team at the next Paralympics.

4 We want to use product place ______________ and show our mobile phone in a Bond film.

5 I work as a software develop ______________ for a computer company.

# Advertising

| | | |
|---|---|---|
| **to admit** | to confess, | zugeben, gestehen |
| **commercial break** | pause between TV shows when adverts are shown | Werbepause |
| **to cut** | to get rid of sth | ausblenden |
| **decline** | decrease | Rückgang |
| **to decrease** | to go down | fallen, sinken |
| **to drop** | to fall | fallen |
| **to drown in** | to be surrounded by | ertränken in |
| **to exaggerate** | *n* exaggeration | übertreiben |
| **to fail** | to be unsuccessful | versagen |
| **to go bankrupt** | to no longer have enough money to pay off your debts | in Konkurs gehen, Pleite gehen |
| **gradual(ly)** | slowly over a period of time | allmählich |
| **hard sell** | selling technique that puts a lot of pressure on the customer | aggressive Verkaufstechnik |
| **to increase** | to go up | steigen, zunehmen |
| **to lighten up** | to feel less worried | aufheitern |
| **lively** | fun | lebhaft |
| **one-sided** | showing only one aspect of a situation | einseitig |
| **rapid** | quick | schnell |
| **to recover** | to return to normal, to get better | sich erholen |
| **to remain** | to stay the same | bleiben |
| **soft sell** | selling technique that doesn't put pressure on the customer | zurückhaltende Verkaufstechnik |
| **to stand for sth** | to mean | für etwas stehen |
| **steady, steadily** | even(ly) | stetig |
| **terrible** | awful | schrecklich, furchtbar |
| **word of mouth** | *phr* to spread by word of mouth | Mundpropaganda |

## 1 What do the underlined words or phrases mean? Choose the correct definition.

1 I usually make tea in the commercial break.

- ☐ a a break in a television programme in which advertising is shown
- ☐ b when you take time off work to do something for yourself
- ☐ c a great career opportunity

2 They found our company by word of mouth.

- ☐ a They saw our advertising and decided to phone us.
- ☐ b People recommended our company to them.
- ☐ c People on the street told them how to find our office.

3 etc. stands for etcetera

- ☐ a to mean the opposite of
- ☐ b to be similar to
- ☐ c to mean the same as

## 2 Complete the crossword with the opposite of the words below.

1 increase
2 change
3 understate
4 succeed
5 rapid
6 get worse

# Media madness

| | | |
|---|---|---|
| **abuse** | *v* to abuse sb | Anpöbelung, Beschimpfung(en) |
| **to apologize** | *n* apology | entschuldigen |
| **audience** | viewers of a TV show/film/etc. | Zuschauer |
| **background** | origin | Hintergrund |
| **to behave** | *n* behaviour | sich benehmen |
| **to blame sb** | to think that sb is responsible for sth | die Schuld geben, verantwortlich machen |
| **celebrity** | sb famous | Promi(nente/r) |
| **clash** | conflict | Konflikt, Zusammenstoß |
| **charity** | *phr* an act of charity | wohltätiger Verein |
| **contact** | *phr* to stay in contact | Kontakt, Verbindung |
| **contestant** | sb taking part in a contest | Kandidat/in |
| **embarrassing** | *v* to embarrass | peinlich |
| **entertaining** | *n* entertainment | unterhaltsam |
| **to exploit** | *n* exploitation | be-, ausnutzen |
| **face-to-face contact** | close contact | persönlicher Kontakt |
| **fame** | *adj* famous | Ruhm |
| **latest news** | things that have happened recently | neueste, letzte Neuigkeit(en), Nachricht(en) |
| **to launch** | to begin, to start | starten |
| **long-running** | e.g. a long-running TV show | mit langer Laufzeit |
| **maker** | person who makes sth | Macher/in, Produzent/in |
| **personality** | a person's character | Persönlichkeit |
| **popular press** | media that aims to reach a wide audience | Boulevardpresse |
| **public** | in front of other people | öffentlich |
| **to raise** | *phr* to raise money for sth | sammeln |
| **to react** | *n* reaction | reagieren |
| **to throw out** | to force sb to leave | hinauswerfen |
| **viewer** | person who watches a TV programme | Zuschauer/in |

**1** **Read the text and work out the anagrams.**

## 8 p.m.

**BBC 1: Benders**

A special two hour episode of Britain's longest NIRUNNG[1] soap opera. In last week's dramatic episode Jim finally realized that Adam was stealing money from Jos. Adam phones Jim to PGZIAOOLE[2] for behaving so badly. Will Jim forgive him?

**BBC 2: Celebrity challenges**

More embarrassment for Dan Dolly's TCLEEBIRY[3] contestants. This week actress Sheila Marley and TV presenter Douglas Scott take part in a series of tough challenges designed by the DUAEICNE[4] such as trying to eat yoghurt with a knife and fork or riding a bicycle backwards. Don't try these challenges at home!

**ITV: ITV News**

Jenny Brown presents a summary of the TALETS[5] news, sport and entertainment from around the world followed by a special CKABORGUDN[6] report on young stars and the effects of fame on their lives. Hayley Mine interviews filmmaker Louis Browne about his response to accusations that he PIOXELST[7] young actors hoping for a career in the movie industry.

**Channel 4: Classmates**

Tonight is the AULNHC[8] of Chris Mardy's new show, in which he reunites people who have not been in contact for many years. We meet Alison Bowle and her old French teacher who she has not seen for twenty years. At school the two had a big personality LACSH[9] and Alison played many cruel tricks on her teacher. Now Alison wants to say sorry. The studio audience and WIEVRES[10] at home can enjoy watching their reactions as they come face-to-face with each other after twenty years!

# Media madness

| | | |
|---|---|---|
| **at risk** | in danger of | gefährdet |
| **to avoid** | to try not to do sth | (ver)meiden |
| **to bet** | to be sure that | wetten |
| **to be worried** | to be afraid of what might happen | befürchten |
| **careful** | *phr* to be careful | vorsichtig |
| **circle of** | *phr* circle of friends | Kreis von |
| **component** | part | Bestandteil |
| **to emphasize** | *n* emphasis | betonen, hervorheben |
| **experience** | *phr* to have experience of sth | Erfahrung |
| **honest** | truthful | ehrlich |
| **lazy** | *n* laziness | faul |
| **to lie** | <> to tell the truth | lügen |
| **to make no sense** | to be hard to understand | nicht sinnvoll sein |
| **out loud** | so that other people can hear | laut vernehmlich |
| **over the top** | too much | übertrieben |
| **to pay attention to** | to be careful with | beachten, achten auf |
| **polite** | <> rude | unhöflich |
| **provider** | *v* to provide | Anbieter |
| **range** | *phr* a wide range of | Reihe, Spektrum |
| **researcher** | *v* to research sth | Forscher/in |
| **to shorten** | to make sth shorter | (ver)kürzen |
| **to shout** | to speak very loudly | schreien, verkünden |
| **to shut up** | *(inf)* to be quiet | den Mund halten |
| **stranger** | sb you don't know | Fremde/r |
| **thief** | sb who steals | Dieb/in |
| **unnecessary** | <> necessary | unnötig |
| **unusual** | strange | ungewöhnlich |
| **user** | person who uses sth | Anwender/in, Benutzer/in |

## 1 Fill in the gaps with one of the words below. There are two words you don't need.

avoiding | at risk | careful | shout | stranger | truth | rude | thief | honest | lazy | danger | lied

1 Who's that man sitting at Katie's desk. He's a complete ________________ to me.

2 A ________________ ran off with my mobile phone yesterday.

3 You're so ________________! You just sit at home watching TV all day!

4 - Here, you dropped some money. - Oh, thank you for being so ________________.

5 She was very ________________ to the boss and told him to shut up!

6 Several species of bird are ________________ due to environmental damage.

7 I haven't seen Liam for two days now. I think he's ________________ seeing me.

8 Be ________________! There's broken glass on the floor.

9 You don't need to ________________! I'm standing right next to you!

10 He ________________ to me. He said he loved me but he was with another woman.

## 2 Match the sentences which mean the same thing.

1 I don't understand.
2 Pay attention in class.
3 I hope she's OK.
4 He's very popular.
5 Read it out loud.
6 That is obviously wrong.
7 I bet it'll rain again tomorrow.
8 80 euros for a T-shirt! That's too expensive!

a I'm worried about her.
b Do it so that everybody can hear you.
c The price is over the top.
d It doesn't make any sense.
e I really think that's what will happen.
f He has a large circle of friends.
g Listen to the teacher.
h Number 1 is clearly the wrong answer.

# Advertising & media

| | | |
|---|---|---|
| **advertising agency** | a company which plans advertising campaigns | Werbeagentur |
| **box office hit** | a very successful film | Kassenschlager |
| **broadsheet** | a serious newspaper | großformatige Zeitung |
| **circulation** | usual number of copies of a newspaper sold | Auflage |
| **consumer** | *v* to consume | Verbraucher/in |
| **expenditure** | money spent, e.g. on a campaign | Ausgabe(n) |
| **footage** | e.g. video footage | Filmmaterial |
| **gap in the market** | the chance to sell a product which isn't available yet | Marktlücke |
| **glossy magazine** | an expensive magazine with lots of photographs | Hochglanzillustrierte |
| **headline** | the main title of an article | Schlagzeile, Überschrift |
| **hype** | *phr* media hype | Rummel |
| **lead article** | the main article in a newspaper or magazine | Leitartikel |
| **prime time** | *phr* prime-time television | Hauptsendezeit |
| **market research** | finding out information about the market | Marktforschung |
| **niche product** | a product made for a small section of the market | Nischenprodukt |
| **plot** | the storyline of a film / book | Handlung |
| **ratings** | *v* to rate sth (a film, book) | Werte, Bewertung, Quote |
| **revenue** | money earned by a business | Einkünfte, Einnahmen |
| **sensationalist** | scandalous | Sensations- |
| **supplement** | extra part of a newspaper, e.g. travel, literature | Beilage |
| **tabloid** | a sensationalist newspaper | Boulevardblatt |
| **TV licence** | a fee paid for receiving TV broadcasts | Fernsehlizenz |
| **watershed** | the time after which programmes unsuitable for children can be shown | Zeitpunkt, bis zu dem nur jugendfreie Fernsehsendungen ausgestrahlt werden sollen |

## 1 Sort these words into the categories.

box office hit
circulation
broadsheet
ratings
headline
watershed
supplement
footage
lead article
tabloid
plot

| Press | TV and film |
|---|---|
| | |

## 2 Circle the correct word to complete the sentences.

1 The series is going to be shown on *prime-time / lead-time / best-time* TV.

2 You can't buy a product like this anywhere! We've found a *gap / hole / place* in the market.

3 This series is too violent. We'll have to show it after the *borderline / watershed / closure*.

4 If you have a TV at home, you have to pay a TV *payment / fee / licence*.

5 Tabloids often print *sensible / sensationalist / glossy* articles.

6 Not many consumers buy this kind of thing. It's a real *corner / edge / niche* product.

# On the move

| | | |
|---|---|---|
| **amazed** | *n* amazement | erstaunt |
| **annoyed** | *v* to annoy sb | verärgert |
| **anxious** | *n* anxiety | besorgt, beunruhigt |
| **car sharing** | sharing a car to reduce costs/pollution etc. | gemeinsame Pkw-Nutzung |
| **commuter** | *v* to commute | Pendler/in |
| **delighted** | *n* delight | (sehr) erfreut, entzückt |
| **disappointed** | *n* disappointment | enttäuscht |
| **extent** | *phr* to a certain extent | (Aus-)Maß, Umfang, Grad |
| **fortune** | *phr* to cost a fortune | Vermögen |
| **frustrated** | *n* frustration | frustriert |
| **gas** | *(AE) BE:* petrol | Benzin, Treibstoff |
| **gridlock** | situation where there are so many cars none can move | Totalstau |
| **government** | *v* to govern | Regierung |
| **motorway** | *(BE) AE:* highway | Autobahn |
| **nervous** | *n* nervousness | nervös |
| **nursery** | *phr* day nursery, nursery school | Kindertagestätte, Kita |
| **pleased** | *v* to please sb | froh, erfreut |
| **shocked** | *n* shock | schockiert |
| **state** | e.g. California, Kentucky | (Bundes-)Staat |
| **suburb** | *adj* suburban | Vorort, Außenbezirk |
| **surprised** | *n* surprise | überrascht, erstaunt |
| **tailback** | long line of still or slow-moving traffic | Autoschlange |
| **terrified** | very scared | erschrocken |
| **traffic jam** | *phr* to be stuck in a traffic jam | (Verkehrs-)Stau |
| **transport** | *phr* means of transport | Verkehr(smittel) |
| **truck** | *(AE) BE:* lorry | Lastwagen, Lkw |
| **upset** | unhappy | bestürzt, entsetzt |
| **various** | a range of | verschieden |

**1** **Find eight words which describe feelings in the puzzle below. Are the feelings positive, negative or neutral? Sort them into categories.**

| | | | | | | | | | | | |
|---|---|---|---|---|---|---|---|---|---|---|---|
| G | J | K | E | W | A | C | B | S | K | L | G |
| H | A | M | A | Z | E | D | F | U | D | R | F |
| S | H | O | C | K | E | D | Z | R | E | H | D |
| T | R | G | P | H | J | A | L | P | L | S | A |
| W | Q | E | L | G | S | N | D | R | I | A | Y |
| C | V | G | E | J | H | N | I | I | G | D | S |
| A | J | P | A | L | D | O | E | S | H | W | P |
| S | U | P | S | E | T | Y | G | E | T | F | Z |
| R | E | O | E | K | L | E | F | D | E | S | V |
| H | U | R | D | W | O | D | A | S | D | W | P |
| T | R | U | S | T | R | A | T | E | D | H | F |
| C | V | B | H | Z | T | R | S | Y | M | O | P |

| **Positive** | **Negative** | **Neutral** |
|---|---|---|
| ______________ | ______________ | ______________ |
| ______________ | ______________ | ______________ |
| | ______________ | |
| | ______________ | |

**2** **Match the words which have the same meaning in British and American English.**

| **British English** | **American English** |
|---|---|
| 1 petrol | a highway |
| 2 lorry | b kindergarten |
| 3 motorway | c gas |
| 4 nursery school | d state |
| 5 county | e truck |

# On the move

| | | |
|---|---|---|
| **to benefit from** | *adj* beneficial | Nutzen ziehen aus, profitieren von |
| **boot** | *(BE) AE*: trunk | Kofferraum |
| **to calculate** | *n* calculation | kalkulieren, berechnen |
| **to combine** | *n* combination | (sich) verbinden |
| **congestion charging** | money you have to pay to drive in a city centre | Staugebühr |
| **to destroy** | *n* destruction | zerstören, vernichten |
| **development** | progress | Entwicklung |
| **electricity** | *adj* electric, electrical | Elektrizität, Strom |
| **engine** | part of vehicle that produces power to move | Motor |
| **environmentalist** | person who wants to protect the environment | Umweltschützer/in |
| **environmentally friendly** | not harmful to the environment | umweltfreundlich |
| **to estimate** | *n* estimation | schätzen |
| **in common** | *phr* to have sth in common | gemeinsam |
| **to manufacture** | to produce | herstellen, produzieren |
| **movement** | *v* to move | Bewegung |
| **owner** | person who owns | Besitzer/in |
| **to plug into** | to connect equipment to the electricity supply | einstöpseln, sich anschließen an |
| **poor** | not good | schlecht, mangelhaft |
| **to recharge** | *adj* rechargeable | aufladen |
| **reduction** | *v* to reduce | Verringerung, Senkung |
| **renewable** | *phr* renewable energy | erneuerbar |
| **rush hour** | time when the roads are busy | Hauptverkehrszeit, Berufsverkehr |
| **speed** | *phr* at a high/low speed | Geschwindigkeit |
| **vehicle** | e.g. car, bus, truck | Fahrzeug |
| **unless** | if not | wenn nicht |
| **waste** | *phr* waste product | Abfall |

## 1 What do the <u>underlined</u> words or phrases mean? Choose the correct definition.

1 Jenny and I have a lot <u>in common</u>.

- ☐ a Jenny and I are not friends.
- ☐ b Jenny and I have a lot of similar interests.
- ☐ c Jenny and I have ordinary names.

2 Wind power is a type of <u>renewable</u> energy.

- ☐ a It is a type of energy that can be used up.
- ☐ b It is a type of energy that can not be used up.
- ☐ c It is a type of energy that has never been used before.

3 London has an expensive <u>congestion charging</u> scheme.

- ☐ a Motorists have to pay if they cause a traffic jam in London.
- ☐ b Motorists have to pay if they enter the centre of London in their vehicle.
- ☐ c Motorists have to charge their passengers money if they drive in the centre of London.

## 2 Complete the sentences with the English equivalents of the German words in brackets.

1 I think the children will ______________________ *(profitieren von)* a weekend in the countryside.

2 It's cheaper to go by bus. There is ______________________ *(eine Staugebühr)* in the city centre.

3 I'll put your bags in the ______________________ *(Kofferraum)* of the taxi.

4 The underground was really full. It must have been ______________________ *(Hauptverkehrszeit)*.

5 I only bought the printer two weeks ago and it's broken already. It must be really ______________________ *(mangelhafte)* quality.

6 They have started using ______________________ *(umweltfreundliche)* packaging.

7 There was a power cut last night. We didn't have any ______________________ (*Strom*) for five hours!

8 Susie is a good friend of mine. We have a lot of things ______________________ *(gemeinsam)*.

9 The policeman asked me to move my ______________________ *(Fahrzeug)* immediately.

10 This car is so old, I think it needs a new ______________________ *(Motor)*.

# 5 Green enough?

| | | |
|---|---|---|
| **amount** | quantity | Menge |
| **average** | typical | normal, durchschnittlich |
| **benefit** | advantage | Nutzen, Vorteil |
| **brief** | quick, for a short time | kurz |
| **building** | *v* to build | Gebäude |
| **bulb** | *phr* light bulb | Glühbirne, -lampe |
| **destruction** | *v* to destroy | Zerstörung, Vernichtung |
| **disaster** | *phr* a natural diasaster | Katastrophe, Unglück |
| **epidemic** | outbreak of a disease or illness | Epidemie |
| **to face** | *phr* to face problems | sich gegenübersehen |
| **flood** | a large amount of water covering an area that is usually dry | Flut, Überschwemmung |
| **to get fit** | to become healthy and strong by exercising | fit werden |
| **to get rid of** | to give away or remove sth | abschaffen |
| **insulation** | *phr* wall insulation | Isolierung |
| **low-energy** | something that uses very little power | Niedrigenergie-, Spar- |
| **matter** | situation, problem | Sache, Ding, Angelegenheit |
| **to meet needs** | to satisfy a requirement | Bedürfnisse decken |
| **mixture** | combination | Mischung |
| **natural** | <> man-made | natürlich |
| **previous** | before | vorher (gehend) |
| **progress** | *phr* to make progress | Fortschritt/e |
| **report** | *v* to report | Bericht, Reportage |
| **roof** | e.g. the roof of the house | Dach |
| **to run out of** | e.g. to run out of money | ausgehen |
| **storm** | *phr* a severe storm | Unwetter, Sturm |
| **strength** | *adj* strong | Kraft, Stärke |
| **to turn down** | *phr* to turn down the music | herunterregeln |
| **unreliable** | <> reliable | unzuverlässig |

## 1 Complete the sentences with words from the list on page 35.

1 It was the worst ______________________ we've had in years. The whole village was under water.

2 If we had better wall ______________________, it wouldn't be so cold in here.

3 We're making ______________________ with the problem but there's still a long way to go.

4 She's not very ______________________: she often says she'll visit me and then doesn't.

5 We need to ______________________ the problem, not try and forget that it exists.

6 It's really hot in here. Can you ______________________ the heating, please?

7 My new car was so expensive I nearly ______________________ of money to pay the bills.

8 There's been a bit of a flu ______________________. Everyone seems to be ill!

9 It's just a ______________________ article – it shouldn't take long to read it.

10 It's a lot colder than it normally is at this time of year. The ______________________ temperature is 10°C, but today it's only 2°C.

## 2 Match the words to the phrasal verbs. Sometimes there es more than one possibility.

run out of: ______________________________________________

turn down: ______________________________________________

get rid of: ______________________________________________

the evidence | the music | an offer | debts | milk | ideas | an old sweater | an applicant | a problem | cash | light bulbs | a headache | the oven | the heating | energy

# 5 Green enough?

| | | |
|---|---|---|
| **to act** | *n* action | handeln |
| **century** | 100 years | Jahrhundert |
| **climate** | weather | Klima |
| **danger** | <> safety | Gefahr |
| **to delay** | *n* delay | aufschieben, hinauszögern |
| **desperate** | urgent | verzweifelt |
| **to disappear** | to vanish, to be gone | verschwinden |
| **to drown in** | to be surrounded by | ertränken in |
| **economy** | *phr* the world economy | Wirtschaft |
| **essential** | vital, necessary, important | notwendig, wesentlich |
| **to fight** | *n* fight | bekämpfen |
| **impossible** | <> possible | unmöglich |
| **level** | amount | Niveau |
| **to melt** | <> to freeze | schmelzen |
| **moreover** | also | außerdem, zudem |
| **nuclear** | e.g. nuclear weapons | Atom- |
| **to owe** | *phr* to owe sb money | verdanken, schulden |
| **possibility** | *adj* possible | Möglichkeit |
| **to prevent** | to stop sth from happening | verhindern, verhüten |
| **rare** | <> common | selten |
| **to reduce** | *n* reduction | reduzieren, verringern |
| **to respond to** | to give an answer | reagieren auf |
| **severe** | very bad | ernst, schwer, stark |
| **stormy** | *n* storm | stürmisch |
| **success** | *adj* successful | Erfolg |
| **sudden** | *adj* suddenly | plötzlich |
| **target** | goal | Ziel(vorgaben), Soll(zahlen) |
| **thanks to** | because of | dank |
| **twice** | two times | zweimal, doppelt |
| **vision** | goal | Vision, Vorausschau |
| **to warn** | *n* warning | warnen |

**1** **Read the comments about environmental issues and replace the underlined words with words which have a similar meaning.**

**1** I think we need to <u>do something</u> now to <u>prevent</u> further global warning.

**2** Scientists have been <u>telling</u> us for years about the dangers of the melting Arctic ice. It's time to do something about it.

**3** <u>Because of</u> greedy politicians, factories are producing more pollution than ever.

**4** The <u>level</u> of carbon dioxide in the air isn't as high as everybody thinks. It's all exaggerated.

**5** <u>Severe</u> weather is hitting Europe more and more often and that's scary.

1 ______________________ 4 ______________________

2 ______________________ 5 ______________________

3 ______________________

**2** **Find the words which have the opposite meaning. There are two words you don't need.**

rare possible safety danger melt global nuclear common freeze impossible

Extra Vocabulary

# Transport & environment

| | | |
|---|---|---|
| **acid rain** | rain which contains harmful chemicals | saurer Regen |
| **aircraft** | e.g. plane, helicopter, etc. | Flugzeug |
| **deforestation** | <> reforestation | Abholzung, Entwaldung |
| **to dump** | *phr* to dump chemical waste | abladen, auskippen |
| **to die out** | to become extinct | aussterben |
| **ecosystem** | plants, animals and insects and their environment | Ökosystem |
| **famine** | when a large percentage of a population has no food | Hungersnot |
| **to fell** | to cut down a tree | fällen |
| **forest fire** | when a large number of trees burn down | Waldbrand |
| **to generate** | to produce | erzeugen |
| **global warming** | increases in the earth's temperature caused by pollution | Erderwärmung, Treibhauseffekt |
| **green energy** | renewable energy | grüne Energie |
| **insufficient** | not enough | ungenügend |
| **lane** | *phr* a three lane motorway | (Fahr-)Spur, Weg |
| **natural resources** | e.g. sun, wind, etc. | natürliche Ressourcen |
| **oil spill** | accident in which oil from a tanker goes into the sea | Ölverschmutzung |
| **organic** | e.g. organic farming | organisch, Bio- |
| **over-fishing** | taking too many fish out of a river or sea | Überfischung |
| **to preserve** | *n* preservation | bewahren, erhalten |
| **rainforest** | tropical forest, e.g. the Amazon | Regenwald |
| **runway** | length of ground used by aeroplanes to take off | Start-, Landebahn |
| **unleaded petrol** | <> leaded petrol | bleifreies Benzin |
| **wildlife** | animals and birds which live in the natural world | Tierwelt |

## 1 Match the words or phrases which go together.

| | | | |
|---|---|---|---|
| 1 | green | a | petrol |
| 2 | unleaded | b | resources |
| 3 | over- | c | fishing |
| 4 | organic | d | fire |
| 5 | natural | e | warming |
| 6 | forest | f | farming |
| 7 | acid | g | rain |
| 8 | global | h | energy |

## 2 Replace the underlined words with one of the words below. There are more words than you need.

dump · lane · runway · insufficient · wildlifc · felled · deforestation · famine · reforestation

1 Some parts of the world are already suffering because of higher temperatures and not enough rainfall.

2 Hundreds of acres of rainforest are cut down every day.

3 The animal and bird population has been affected by light pollution from nearby towns.

4 The authorities now have a policy of planting new trees in areas where forests have been destroyed.

5 Some irresponsible companies still throw away chemical waste into rivers and lakes.

6 Houses have been knocked down to build a new six-row motorway.

7 Local residents complained about the building of a new piece of ground for aeroplanes to take off at Heathrow Airport.

# 6 Modern ways to work

| | | |
|---|---|---|
| **airline** | company which flies planes | Fluggesellschaft |
| **challenging** | *v* to challenge sb | herausfordernd, anstrengend |
| **clerk** | a worker in charge of accounts, records, etc. | (Bank-)Angestellte/r |
| **company benefits** | e.g. healthcare, paid holiday, etc. | Firmenvergünstigungen |
| **CV** | *(abbrev)* Curriculum Vitae | Lebenslauf |
| **dead-end** | *phr* a dead-end job | ohne Perspektiven |
| **to deal with** | to take care of sth | sich befassen mit, zu tun haben mit |
| **employer** | <> employee | Arbeitgeber/in |
| **expenses** | costs | Kosten, Ausgaben |
| **factory** | building where things are made | Fabrik |
| **flight attendant** | person who looks after passengers on an aeroplane | Flugbegleiter/in, Steward/ess |
| **to hire** | to recruit | anstellen |
| **instructor** | person who gives instructons | Lehrer/in, Ausbilder/in |
| **qualification** | certificate of training or learning | Qualifikation, Fähigkeit |
| **receptionist** | sb who works in a reception | Empfangsdame, -chef |
| **redundant** | made unemployed | arbeitslos, freigesetzt |
| **repetitive** | *v* to repeat | monoton |
| **salary** | amount of money earned | Gehalt, Lohn |
| **secretarial course** | course on how to become a secretary | Sekretariatskurs |
| **temporary** | <> permanent | zeitlich befristet |
| **travel agent** | person who organizes holidays and transport | Reiseverkehrskaufmann/-frau |
| **varied** | *v* to vary | abwechslungsreich |
| **vocational** | *n* vocation | in der beruflichen Ausbildung |

## 1 Complete the puzzle to find the hidden job.

1 to look after, to take care of (*2 words*)
2 not permanent
3 often the first person you speak to when you go into a company's office
4 to do with jobs
5 many different things
6 somebody who arranges holidays as a job (2 words)
7 somebody who teaches you how to do something
8 the money you get paid for a job

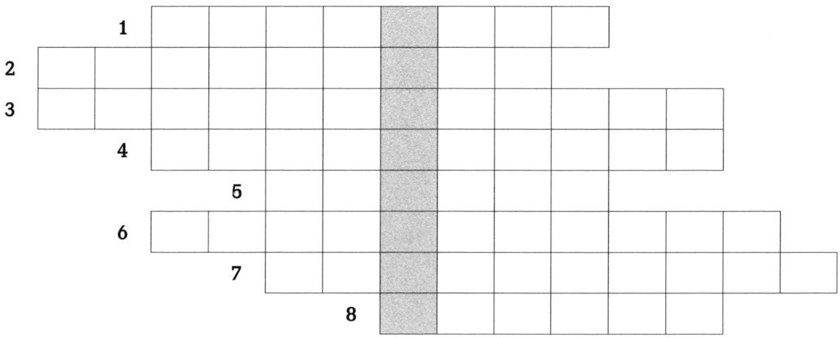


## 2 Find the odd one out. Give a reason for your choice.

1 challenging - repetitive -employer - varied

_______________________________________________

2 company benefits - salary - money - expenses

_______________________________________________

3 clerk - secretary - flight attendant - travel agent

_______________________________________________

4 secretary - airline - factory - travel agency

_______________________________________________

# Modern ways to work

| | | |
|---|---|---|
| **cafeteria** | place where you can get food in factories, hospitals, etc. | Kantine (mit Selbstbedienung) |
| **commitment** | *v* to commit | Einsatz, Engagement |
| **conclusion** | summary | (Schluss-)Folgerung |
| **contract** | a formal document or agreement | (Arbeits-)Vertrag |
| **creche facilities** | place where babies and small children are cared for | Krippeneinrichtungen |
| **to develop** | *n* development | (sich) entwickeln |
| **employee** | *v* to employ | Arbeitnehmer/in, Beschäftigte/r |
| **fringe benefits** | e.g. pension, insurance, holiday, etc. | zusätzliche Sozialleistungen |
| **generous** | *n* generosity | großzügig |
| **healthcare** | service providing medical treatment | medizinische Versorgung |
| **to invest** | *n* investment | investieren |
| **law** | rules of a country or organization | Gesetz |
| **maternity leave** | paid time off from work for new mothers | Mutterschaftsurlaub |
| **membership** | e.g. gym membership | Mitgliedschaft |
| **paternity leave** | paid time off from work for new fathers | Vaterschaftsurlaub |
| **prospects** | chances of being successful | Aussichten |
| **reply** | *v* to reply | Antwort, Erwiderung, Reaktion |
| **resource** | reserve | Reserve, Ressource |
| **subsidized** | *v* to subsidize | subventioniert |
| **travel insurance** | insurance in case of theft, illness, etc. on holiday | Reiseversicherung |
| **terms** | e.g. terms of a contract | Bedingungen, Konditionen |
| **valuable** | *n* value | wertvoll |
| **white-collar** | connected with work in an office | Schreibtisch-, Büro- |
| **workforce** | the workers | Belegschaft |

## 1 Find the words which go together.

| | | | |
|---|---|---|---|
| 1 | gym | a | insurance |
| 2 | fringe | b | membership |
| 3 | travel | c | facilities |
| 4 | paternity | d | treatment |
| 5 | creche | e | benefits |
| 6 | medical | f | leave |

## 2 Work out the anagrams.

1 somebody who receives a regular salary from a company: OMELEPEY

______________________________

2 where company workers have lunch: FEARCETIA

______________________________

3 to continuously improve something: EEVPODL

______________________________

4 hard work and loyalty to a company or project: MOCINETMMT

______________________________

5 to give a lot of time, energy or money to make something successful: ENIVTS

______________________________

## 3 Fill in the gaps with the English equivalents of the German words in brackets.

1 The manufacturers had to make half their ______________ (*Belegschaft*) redundant.

2 I thanked my grandfather for his ______________ (*Großzügigkeit*).

3 My team usually eats together in the company ______________ (*Kantine*) at lunchtime.

4 Read the ______________ (*Bedingungen*) of the ______________ (*Vertrag*) carefully before you sign it.

5 Our company offers ______________ (*subventioniert*) healthcare.

# Going global

| | | |
|---|---|---|
| **acceptable** | *v* to accept | annehmbar, akzeptabel |
| **amusing** | funny, entertaining | lustig, amüsant |
| **to be required to** | *n* requirement | müssen |
| **cutting-edge** | very modern | Spitzen-, Hightech-, modern |
| **data** | facts and figures | Daten |
| **directed at** | aimed at | gerichte auf, abzielend auf |
| **dishonest** | <> honest | unehrlich |
| **to dominate** | to have command or influence over | dominieren |
| **efficient** | competent | effizient, (leistungs)fähig |
| **equipment** | the things necessary for a particular kind of job | Ausrüstung |
| **excuse** | *phr* to make an excuse | Ausrede, Entschuldigung |
| **explanation** | reason | Erklärung |
| **goods** | merchandise | Ware(n), Güter |
| **offshore** | in another country | ins/im Ausland |
| **opportunity** | chance | Chance, Möglichkeit |
| **order** | *v* to order | Bestellung, Auftrag |
| **overtime** | *phr* to do overtime | Überstunden |
| **paycheck** | *(AE) BE:* salary cheque | Gehalt(sscheck) |
| **pleasant** | friendly and polite | angenehm, nett, freundlich |
| **rarely** | not often | selten |
| **to redevelop** | to restore | erneuern, neu entwickeln |
| **to sack** | to fire | entlassen, feuern |
| **sensitive** | being easily affected by sth | empfindlich |
| **to shake** | *phr* to shake hands | schütteln |
| **staff** | a group of workers or employees | Angestellte, Mitarbeiter/innen |
| **to trust** | to believe or have confidence in sth or sb | vertrauen |
| **uncomfortable** | uneasy | ungemütlich, unwohl |

## 1 Replace the underlined words with one of the words or phrases below.

an opportunity | felt uncomfortable | done overtime | amusing | explanation | made an excuse | paycheck | rarely saw | ordered | they shook hands | cutting-edge | pleasant

1 Sara got her <u>months' wages</u>.

2 She had <u>worked extra hours</u> and had more money.

3 She wanted to go to a <u>new and exciting</u> band's concert.

4 She <u>bought</u> the tickets online.

5 There was a party afterwards: <u>a chance</u> to meet the band!

6 But at the party she <u>didn't feel relaxed</u>.

7 Then one of the band members, Joe, came over and <u>gave her his hand</u>.

8 At first he was very <u>nice</u> and <u>funny</u>. But he just didn't stop talking...

9 So she <u>lied to him</u> and said she had to go home.

10 She called a friend who she <u>didn't see very often</u> and she invited her to a disco.

11 The disco was fun but then she saw Joe... What <u>reason</u> could she give for being there?

# Going global

| | | |
|---|---|---|
| **to bury** | *phr* to bury your dreams | begraben |
| **casual** | occasional | Gelegenheits- |
| **to climb** | to rise | klettern, steigen |
| **concern** | worry | Sorge, Interesse, Anliegen |
| **to despair** | to lose hope | verzweifeln |
| **earnings** | money made | Einkünfte |
| **to examine** | to look at sth carefully | untersuchen, prüfen |
| **export** | selling of goods to another country | Ausfuhr, Export |
| **guaranteed** | secured, definite | garantiert |
| **to identify** | to find | herausfinden |
| **middlemen** | people in the middle of the supply chain | Zwischenhändler |
| **to offload** | unload | weitergeben |
| **picker** | *v* to pick | Pflücker/in |
| **poverty** | *adj* poor | Armut |
| **precarious** | risky | unsicher, prekär |
| **producer** | sb who grows or makes goods and materials | Produzent/in, Erzeuger |
| **to relate to** | to connect | sich beziehen auf |
| **to rely on** | to depend on | angewiesen sein auf |
| **security** | stability | Sicherheit |
| **to seek** | to look for | suchen |
| **shareholder** | sb who owns stocks in a company | Aktionär/in |
| **strength** | *adj* strong | Stärke |
| **sub-contractor** | | Subunternehmer |
| **supply chain** | chain through which products are distributed from producer to retailer | Versorgungskette |
| **target** | goal | Ziel(vorgaben), Soll(zahlen) |
| **weakness** | *adj* weak | Schwäche |
| **widely** | *adj* wide | weit (verbreitet) |

**1** **Work out the anagrams to complete the sentences.**

1 Our company LESERI on exports to the Middle East.

______________________________

2 We are NEXMAINGI the situation very carefully.

______________________________

3 By cutting out the DIMMELDNE we have reduced costs quite effectively.

______________________________

4 Please outline your THRENGSTS and KEWANESSSE for us.

______________________________

5 Companies always try to please their DESHAOLSERHR.

______________________________

**2** **Find the missing words to complete the crossword.**

1 When you reach your goal: meet your ...

2 A person who does a job when they are needed, without a contract: ... worker

3 When many customers know your product and think it is good: ... recognized.

4 Some companies promise to lower prices by getting rid of the ...

5 This person works in the fields collecting fruit: fruit ...

6 When you stop dreaming and start to despair about the future, you ... your dreams.

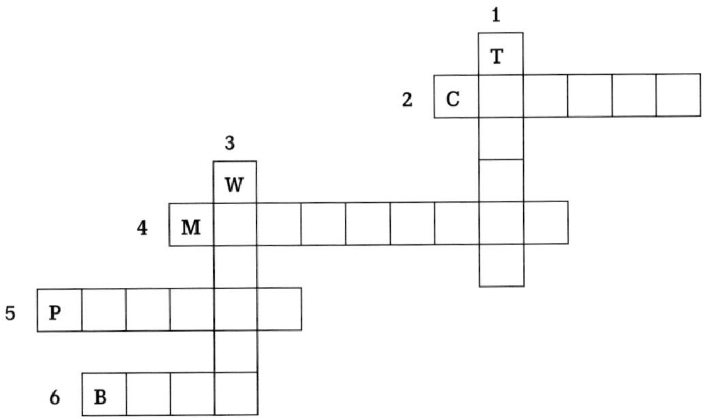

# 8 Finding a job in the EU

| | | |
|---|---|---|
| **ability** | *v* to be able to | Fähigkeit, Können |
| **accommodation** | food and lodging | Unterkunft |
| **to apply for** | e.g. to apply for a job | sich bewerben um |
| **to attach** | *n* attachment | beilegen, -fügen |
| **constitution** | an established arrangement | Verfassung |
| **contribution** | *v* to contribute | Beitrag, Beihilfe |
| **duties** | tasks in a job | Pflichten, Aufgaben |
| **expenses** | *phr* travel expenses | Kosten, Ausgaben |
| **fee** | *phr* admission fee | Gebühr |
| **fluent** | *phr* to be fluent in a language | fließend |
| **headquarters** | main office | Hauptsitz, Zentrale |
| **internship** | work experience in a company | Volontariat |
| **to involve** | to include | einschließen, beinhalten |
| **licence** | *phr* driving licence | Führerschein |
| **outgoing** | e.g. an outgoing personality | kontaktfreudig |
| **practical** | <> theoretical | praktisch |
| **to provide** | to give | zur Verfügung stellen |
| **query** | question | Frage, Rückfrage |
| **to refer to** | to make reference to | sich beziehen auf |
| **referee** | person who writes a job reference | Referenzgeber |
| **reference** | written statement about character and skills | Zeugnis |
| **to reject** | to refuse | ablehnen |
| **to request** | to ask for | fordern |
| **sector** | a particular area of business | Sektor, Bereich |
| **to specialize in** | *n* specialist | sich spezialisieren auf |
| **to submit** | to hand in | einreichen |
| **treaty** | an agreement between countries | Vertrag |
| **vocational** | job-related | beruflich, Berufs- |
| **voter** | *v* to vote | Wähler/in |

## 1 Match the words below to make common expressions.

| | | | |
|---|---|---|---|
| 1 | attach | a | an internship |
| 2 | vocational | b | personality |
| 3 | outgoing | c | training |
| 4 | travel | d | your CV |
| 5 | apply for | e | Spanish |
| 6 | fluent | f | expenses |

## 2 Decide which category the words below belong in and then find it in the word search.

1 answering customer questions, typing letters, writing reports = *duties*

2 service, manufacturing, tourism = s________

3 former employer, trainer, teacher = r________

4 hotel, youth hostel, student flat = a________

5 teamwork, speak good English, drive a car = a________

6 travel, hotel bookings, restaurant bills = e________

| | | | | | | | | | | | | |
|---|---|---|---|---|---|---|---|---|---|---|---|---|
| T | U | R | E | W | A | B | J | L | H | M | O | E |
| N | I | A | B | I | L | I | T | I | E | S | C | X |
| R | O | P | I | K | F | Z | D | A | K | M | U | P |
| E | Z | D | D | S | S | E | C | T | O | R | S | E |
| F | P | O | U | I | U | Z | T | R | E | W | M | N |
| E | S | D | T | F | G | H | J | K | L | Y | O | S |
| R | N | E | I | P | L | M | N | J | I | L | N | E |
| E | Z | G | E | V | C | F | T | R | E | O | E | S |
| E | W | E | S | Q | Y | S | V | P | I | B | Y | T |
| S | T | U | L | O | P | R | F | G | W | A | B | Q |
| A | C | C | O | M | M | O | D | A | T | I | O | N |
| Y | E | K | C | F | I | N | G | A | L | P | N | I |
| U | J | H | Z | T | G | V | W | C | T | O | L | A |
| P | H | U | B | R | E | A | T | C | B | L | V | E |

# 8 Finding a job in the EU

| | | |
|---|---|---|
| **to advise** | *n* advice | raten, beraten |
| **affair** | events or happenings | Angelegenheit |
| **bang** | *phr* to get off with a bang | Paukenschlag |
| **border** | boundary | Grenze, Grenz- |
| **bunch** | *(inf)* a lot of | Gruppe, Haufen |
| **bureaucracy** | *adj* bureaucratic | Bürokratie |
| **corruption** | *v* to corrupt | Korruption |
| **currency** | system of money that a country uses | Währung |
| **to defend** | *n* defence | verteidigen |
| **diverse** | differing from one another | verschieben, unterschiedlich |
| **to evaluate** | to assess | einschätzen, bewerten |
| **frank** | *phr* to be frank with sb | offen, ehrlich |
| **frontier** | boundary | Grenze |
| **to integrate** | *n* integration | sich integrieren |
| **interference** | *v* to interfere | Einmischung |
| **lawyer** | person who has studied law | (Rechts-)Anwalt/Anwältin |
| **legislative** | legal | gesetzgebend |
| **migration** | *v* to migrate | Wanderung(sbewegung) |
| **misleading** | leading in the wrong direction | irreführend |
| **recommendation** | *v* to recommend | Empfehlung |
| **relatively** | quite, somewhat | verhältnismäßig |
| **scarcity** | *adj* scarce | Knappheit |
| **sovereignty** | independent power/authority | Souveränität, Unabhängigkeit |
| **stability** | *adj* stable | Stabilität |
| **take on** | opinion on | Einstellung zu |
| **threat** | sth that is a source of danger | Bedrohung, Drohung |
| **unelected** | <> elected | nicht gewählt |
| **to unite** | to bring together | vereinigen |
| **widening** | increasing in size | Erweiterung |
| **wrongdoing** | dishonest or illegal actions | Fehlverhalten |

## 1 Choose the sentence (a or b) which best describes the meaning of sentences 1 to 5.

1 What's Mandy's take on the affair?

- ☐ a What did Mandy do wrong?
- ☐ b What does Mandy think about the situation?

2 The meeting went relatively well.

- ☐ a The meeting was quite successful.
- ☐ b That was the best meeting I've ever been to.

3 The party got off with a bang.

- ☐ a The party was great right from the start.
- ☐ b The party was really bad from the start.

4 A bunch of kids stood at the door.

- ☐ a Two or three kids stood at the door.
- ☐ b Lots of kids stood at the door.

5 They denied any wrongdoing.

- ☐ a They said that they had done nothing dishonest.
- ☐ b They told the police about the crime.

## 2 The underlined words are related to words in the list. Can you work out their German meanings?

1 Some countries have problems with corrupt politicians.

________________________________________

2 When I have problems, I often ask my aunt for advice.

________________________________________

3 Many people migrated to other countries because of the poor economic situation.

________________________________________

4 The system here is so bureaucratic. I don't want to fill in any more forms!

________________________________________

5 He tried to mislead us with false information.

________________________________________

# Work & globalization

| | | |
|---|---|---|
| **apprentice** | trainee | Auszubildende/r |
| **conference call** | a phone call in which three or more people take part | Telefonkonferenz |
| **corporate** | *n* corporation | Firmen-, Konzern- |
| **free trade zone** | a trading area where there are no taxes to be paid | Freihandelszone |
| **global trade** | <> domestic trade | globaler Handel, Welthandel |
| **to globalize** | to make global | globalisieren |
| **green card** | a visa to live / work in the USA | grüne Karte |
| **high flyer** | sb with the potential to have a very successful career | Senkrechtstarter/in, Hochbegabte(r) |
| **hi-tech** | very technologically advanced | technisch hoch entwickelt |
| **import** | <> export | Import |
| **insourcing** | <> outsourcing | im Inland produzieren |
| **odd jobs** | various kinds of small tasks | Gelegenheitsarbeiten |
| **on the job** | *phr* to train on the job | im Beruf, bei der Arbeit |
| **pay rise** | *phr* to get a pay rise | Gehaltserhöhung |
| **plant** | factory | Werk, Betrieb |
| **professional** | *n* profession | beruflich, fachlich |
| **to promote** | *n* promotion | jdn befördern |
| **to quit** | to stop doing sth, e.g. a job | aufgeben, kündigen |
| **to run** | to manage | betreiben |
| **supervision** | *v* to supervise sb/sth | Aufsicht |
| **sweatshop** | some where people work for low wages in bad conditions | Fabrik mit schlechten Arbeitsbedingungen |
| **to take over** | *n* a takeover | übernehmen |
| **time zone** | one of the areas of the world that has its own time | Zeitzone |
| **trade union** | *(BE) AE:* labor union | Gewerkschaft |
| **work permit** | a document giving permission to work in another country | Arbeitserlaubnis |

## 1 Choose the correct definition of each word or phrase.

1 conference call
- ☐ a official notice requiring all employees to come to a conference
- ☐ b phone call which can involve a number of participants
- ☐ c official speech to open a conference

2 to globalize
- ☐ a to enable your company to operate around the world
- ☐ b to only use global brands in your company
- ☐ c to train your staff in intercultural communication

3 green card
- ☐ a card which states that your company is environmentally friendly
- ☐ b visa for entering a North American country
- ☐ c visa for living and working in the United States

4 trade union
- ☐ a group of businesses which trade amongst each other
- ☐ b organization of workers who look after each other's interests
- ☐ c tariff-free trade between certain countries or regions

## 2 Complete the crossword.

1 trade carried out within the same country or area
2 sb working in a company and learning the skills needed for the job
3 to hire local staff instead of opening a department in a (cheaper) foreign country
4 to be given a higher position in a company
5 to bring goods into your country from abroad
6 place where people work in bad conditions for little money

# 9 Social challenges

| | | |
|---|---|---|
| **abandoned** | deserted | verlassen |
| **addiction** | *v* to be addicted to | Sucht, Abhängigkeit |
| **to bring up** | *n* upbringing | großziehen |
| **to care for sb** | to raise or nurture sb | jdn pflegen, sich um jdn kümmern |
| **to carry on** | to keep going | weitermachen |
| **to catch sb off guard** | to surprise | jdn überraschen, ertappen |
| **childcare** | looking after children | (Kinder-)Erziehung |
| **childminder** | sb who looks after children, e.g. when the parents work | Kinderbetreuer/in, Tagesmutter/-vater |
| **to come to terms with** | to accept | zurechtkommen mit |
| **custom** | social practice or tradition | Brauch |
| **depressing** | very sad | bedrückend, deprimierend |
| **emotional** | e.g. sad, happy, angry, etc. | emotional |
| **ethnic** | connected with origin/race | ethnisch, Volks- |
| **heritage** | e.g. cultural heritage | Erbe, Herkunft |
| **inability** | <> ability | Unfähigkeit |
| **literally** | honestly | buchstäblich |
| **to miss out on** | to not get to do | verpassen |
| **musician** | a person who produces or plays music | Musiker/in |
| **nervous breakdown** | *phr* to have a nervous breakdown | Nervenzusammenbruch |
| **overly** | excessively | übermäßig |
| **peer group** | people who have equal standing in age or class | Gleichaltrige, Clique |
| **rejected** | *v* to reject | abgelehnt |
| **to retire** | to go into retirement | in Rente/Pension gehen |
| **role model** | sb you admire and try to copy | Vorbild |
| **social services** | a state service which deals with family problems | Sozialamt, Sozialdienste |
| **steady** | stable | fest, regelmäßig |
| **tiring** | exhausting | anstrengend, ermüdend |

## 1 Match the words which belong together.

| | | | |
|---|---|---|---|
| 1 | role | a | services |
| 2 | nervous | b | group |
| 3 | peer | c | model |
| 4 | social | d | breakdown |
| 5 | cultural | e | heritage |
| 6 | family | f | upbringing |

## 2 Work out the anagrams.

1 Her father left when she was a teenager. She felt TEDRECJE by him.

______________________________

2 The cat was left alone on the street. It had been DANEDBONA.

______________________________

3 We often went to Mrs Jacob's house after school. She was our NILCIDHMDRE.

______________________________

4 Some migrants find it difficult to get used to the different STUCOMS in their new country.

______________________________

5 We RECAD OFR my brother's children while he was in hospital.

______________________________

6 She was a brilliant CUSIMANI but not very good at organizing her life.

______________________________

7 People often go into TERNERITEM around the age of 65.

______________________________

8 She suffered from a terrible DINADTICO to cocaine.

______________________________

9 We called OACSIL ERSEIVCS because they weren't looking after the child properly.

______________________________

# Social challenges

| | | |
|---|---|---|
| **to achieve** | *n* achievement | erreichen |
| **activist** | sb who actively stands up for a cause or belief | Aktivist/in |
| **air pollution** | *v* to pollute | Luftverschmutzung |
| **arrest** | *v* to arrest sb | Verhaftung, Festnahme |
| **battle** | a conflict or struggle | Kampf |
| **to be concerned with** | to care about, to be interested in | sich befassen mit, sich kümmern um |
| **demo(nstration)** | *v* to demonstrate | Demo(nstration) |
| **disobedience** | misbehaving, breaking rules | Ungehorsam |
| **to extend** | to make bigger | ausweiten, ausbauen |
| **extension** | development | Ausbau |
| **height** | distance from ground upwards | Höhe, Größe |
| **inclusion** | *v* to include | Einbeziehung |
| **logging** | cutting down / removing trees | Abholzung |
| **mainstream** | dominant, popular | vorherrschend(e Meinung) |
| **march** | e.g. protest march | (Protest-)Marsch |
| **nurse** | sb who looks after sick people | Krankenschwester,- pfleger/in |
| **population** | the number of people living in an area | Bevölkerung |
| **powerful** | *n* power | mächtig, stark |
| **priest** | a minister of any religion | Priester/in, Geistliche/r |
| **proportion** | dimenstions or size | Teil, Verhältnis |
| **registered** | *v* to register | registriert, eingetragen |
| **shade** | a different level of opinion or feeling | Schattierung |
| **suffragette** | female supporter of votes for women | Frauenrechtlerin, Suffragette |
| **to summarize** | *n* summary | zusammenfassen |
| **sympathy** | feeling sorry/support for | Mitgefühl, Mitleid |
| **to unite** | to join together | sich vereinigen |
| **urgent** | very important | dringend, eilig |
| **violence** | *adj* violent | Gewalt |

## 1 Complete the text with the English equivalents of the words in brackets.

### Three important women

### Emmeline Pankhurst

This woman was perhaps the most famous ______________________ [1]*(Frauenrechtlerin)* in the initial 'votes for women' movement in Britain. She fought hard for the right of women to vote but her movement was often criticized for using violent methods, such as breaking windows and sometimes setting fire to things. She organized ______________________ [2]*(Protestmärchen)* in London and was ______________________ [3]*(verhaftet)* several times. However, in 1918 British women over 30 gained the right to vote.

### Rosa Parks

On Thursday December 1, 1955, she got on a bus in downtown Montgomery, USA and sat down. At that time, the black ______________________ [4]*(Bevölkerung)* had to sit in a separate part of the bus and had to give up their seats for white people. On this day, Rosa Parks refused to move so that a white person could sit down. The driver called the police and she was arrested and charged with civil ______________________ [5]*(Ungehorsamkeit)*. Many people ______________________ [6]*(sich vereinten)* and stopped using the buses. This protest is known as the Montgomery bus boycott and helped to ______________________ [7]*(erreichen)* the end of black and white separation on Montgomery buses.

### Martina Navratilova

This sportswoman was a ______________________ [8]*(mächtig)* figure in the world of tennis: she was the World Number 1 women's tennis player for seven years in a row and won the most singles matches in tennis history. But tennis matches were not her only ______________________ [9]*(Kampf)*. She fights for gay and lesbian rights and is also ______________________ [10]*(befasst sich mit)* other social problems. She is the inventor of the Rainbow credit card - people give 2% of the amount they spend on the card to gay and lesbian organizations as well as to HIV and breast cancer research.

# Multiculturalism

| | | |
|---|---|---|
| **accompaniment** | *v* to accompany | Begleitung |
| **to be to blame** | he's to blame = it's his fault | an etwas schuld sein |
| **civilisation** | an advanced state of human society | Zivilisation |
| **conflicting** | different | gegensätzlich |
| **conscience** | *phr* to have a guilty conscience | Gewissen |
| **to convince** | to persuade | überzeugen |
| **countless** | so many that they cannot be counted | zahllos |
| **to demand** | to ask in a bold way | (nach)fragen |
| **to deny** | *n* denial | bestreiten |
| **disgust** | repulsion, horror | Ekel |
| **fanatic** | *n* fanaticism | Fanatiker/in |
| **for instance** | for example | zum Beispiel |
| **harsh** | unpleasant | scharf, harsch |
| **headscarf** | worn by Muslim women to cover their heads | Kopftuch |
| **forbidden** | not allowed | verboten |
| **incident** | event | Vorfall, Ereignis |
| **to loosen** | *adj* loose | lockern |
| **monotonous** | to speak in one tone of voice | monoton |
| **perplexed** | confused | perplex, verblüfft |
| **rage** | extreme anger | Wut, Zorn |
| **rowdy** | disorderly | laut, randalierend |
| **sari** | garment worn by Hindu women | Sari (Kleidungsstück) |
| **setting** | scene | Szenerie, Schauplatz |
| **to stare** | to watch sb intensively | starren |
| **temper** | *phr* to lose one's temper | Beherrschung |
| **tie** | garment worn around the neck | Krawatte, Schlips |
| **to tremble** | to shake with fear/nerves/cold | zittern |

## 1 Match the sentences which have the same meaning.

1 I can't stop looking at that man.
2 We missed the train because you didn't get up early enough!
3 Nick was so angry he just started shouting at Lucas.
4 I brought her some flowers after our big argument because I felt bad.
5 I only went to the party because Christine said a famous film star would be there.
6 He said that he hadn't broken her favourite vase.

a He denied that he had done anything wrong.
b I'm staring at him.
c I had a guilty conscience.
d You're to blame.
e He lost his temper with him.
f She convinced me to go.

## 2 Work out the anagrams.

1 The party was so YODRW that the neighbours phoned the police.

_______________

2 He was really boring. His voice was OMOTSONONU.

_______________

3 I was PXRLDEPEE because I didn't understand why she was angry with me.

_______________

4 I was so scared I couldn't stop RETNBMLIG.

_______________

5 He DMEADNDE that I go with him. I had no choice.

_______________

6 It's a great ETSIGTN for a book. The story takes place on a deserted island.

_______________

7 I've seen the film OTSCULNES times. In fact, I can't remember how often I've seen it.

_______________

8 Smoking in the cinema is RFBDOIEDN – you definitely can't do that.

_______________

# 10 Multiculturalism

| | | |
|---|---|---|
| **appeal** | *v* to appeal to (sb/a group) | Anziehungskraft, Anreiz |
| **to apply to** | to count for | gelten/zutreffen für |
| **asset** | a valuable thing to have | Wert, Vorteil |
| **to be willing** | to be inclined/open to | bereit/gewillt sein |
| **to break a law** | to commit a crime | das Gesetz brechen |
| **census** | a population count | (Volks-)Zählung |
| **citizenship** | membership of a country | Staatsbürgerschaft |
| **civil rights** | democratic rights | bürgerliche Rechte |
| **to claim** | to state sth as true | behaupten, erklären |
| **contradictory** | opposite | widersprüchlich |
| **to define** | to describe sth accurately | (sich) definieren |
| **to deport** | *n* deportation | ausweisen, abschieben |
| **to enable** | to help to make possible | (es) ermöglichen |
| **entire** | complete | vollkommen, gänzlich |
| **ethnicity** | race | ethnische Zugehörigkeit |
| **humanitarian** | concerned with human welfare | humanitär |
| **intermarriage** | marriage between people of different races | Mischehe |
| **minority** | <> majority | Minderheit |
| **multiracial** | of many races | ethnisch gemischt |
| **out-dated** | old-fashioned | überholt, veraltet |
| **to outnumber** | to exceed in amount | übertreffen |
| **to reflect** | *n* reflection | widerspiegeln |
| **respondent** | *v* to respond | Befragte/r |
| **segregation** | the separation of different races | Rassentrennung |
| **to shrink** | to get smaller | schrumpfen, zurückgehen |
| **to tolerate** | *n* tolerance | tolerieren |
| **tremendous** | huge | gewaltig |
| **unclear** | <> clear | unklar |
| **uniformity** | *n* uniform | Gleichmäßigkeit |

## 1 Complete the puzzle to find another noun from the list on page 60.

1 when the number of people in a country is counted
2 when everything is the same
3 people from different ethnicities
4 to send someone back to their country of origin
5 what a mirror does
6 the joining of two people from different cultures

| | | | | | |
|---|---|---|---|---|---|
| | | | | | |
| | 2 | 9 | | | |

| | | | | | | |
|---|---|---|---|---|---|---|
| | | | | | | |
| | | | | 5 | | |

| | | | | | | | | | | |
|---|---|---|---|---|---|---|---|---|---|---|
| | | | | | | | | | | |
| | | 10 | | | | | | | | |

| | | | | | |
|---|---|---|---|---|---|
| | | | | | |
| 7 | | 4 | | | |

| | | | | | | | |
|---|---|---|---|---|---|---|---|
| R | | | | | | | |
| 1 | | | | | | | 3 |

| | | | | | | | | | | | | |
|---|---|---|---|---|---|---|---|---|---|---|---|---|
| | | | | | | | | | | | | |
| | 6 | | | | | | | | | | | 8 |

| | | | | | | | | | |
|---|---|---|---|---|---|---|---|---|---|
| R | | | | | | | | | |
| 1 | 2 | 3 | 4 | 5 | 6 | 7 | 8 | 9 | 10 |

## 2 Fill in the gaps with the correct words from the list on page 60.

1 I'm not w__________ to pay that amount of money for such an o__________ model!

2 We need to find ethnically-mixed r__________ for our survey.

3 I think this new game will have t__________ a__________ for teenagers.

4 This new law only a__________ to single mothers.

5 I admitted to my sister that I had put the washing machine on the wrong temperature and s__________ her new jeans.

6 This code should e__________ me to access the network, but it's u__________ where to type it in.

# Crime

| | | |
|---|---|---|
| **abolition** | *v* to abolish | Abschaffung |
| **attempt** | try | Versuch |
| **to be opposed to sth** | to be against sth | gegen etwas sein |
| **burglary** | *n* burglar | Einbruch |
| **capital punishment** | death as punishment | Todesstrafe |
| **clemency** | mercy | Milde, Nachsicht |
| **constitutional** | acceptable to the US Constitution | verfassungsgemäß |
| **to deserve** | *adj* deserving | verdienen |
| **deterrent** | making people not want to do sth | abschreckend |
| **execution** | the act of killing by law as a punishment | Hinrichtung |
| **feminist** | person who supports women's rights | Feministin |
| **fraud** | e.g. bank fraud | Betrug, Unterschlagung |
| **imprisonment** | *v* to imprison sb | Haft, Gefängnis(strafe) |
| **murder** | the crime of killing sb | Mord |
| **prison** | *phr* to send sb to prison | Gefängnis |
| **property** | what sb owns | Eigentum |
| **ransom** | *phr* to pay ransom money | Lösegeld |
| **reformed** | *phr* a reformed criminal | gebessert |
| **rehabilitation** | *v* to rehabilitate sb | Rehabilitation |
| **to reintroduce** | to introduce again | wieder einführen |
| **remorse** | *phr* to show remorse | Reue |
| **to rule** | to decide (legally) | entscheiden |
| **to subject to** | to force sb to suffer sth | unterwerfen, aussetzen |
| **Supreme Court** | highest judicial body in the USA | Oberster Gerichtshof |
| **trivial** | not important | trivial, geringfügig |
| **victim** | *phr* a victim of crime | Opfer |
| **victory** | win | Sieg |

## 1 Put the tiles together to make words which translate the German words below.

| | | | | | | | |
|---|---|---|---|---|---|---|---|
| LARY | MORSE | RE | RAN | CLEM | AT | DER | TIM |
| SOM | BURG | TEMPT | MUR | ~~PUNISH~~ | VIC | ENCY | ~~MENT~~ |

1 Bestrafung punishment
2 Lösegeld ______
3 Nachsicht ______
4 Reue ______
5 Opfer ______
6 Einbruch ______
7 Mord ______
8 Versuch ______

## 2 Find the words which go together.

| | | | |
|---|---|---|---|
| 1 | show | a | punishment |
| 2 | victim of | b | remorse |
| 3 | capital | c | fraud |
| 4 | reformed | d | money |
| 5 | bank | e | crime |
| 6 | ransom | f | criminal |

## 3 Now complete the sentences with the combinations from 2 using the correct forms.

1 I think the state should provide more support for ______.
2 How much ______ are they demanding from the family?
3 They didn't find out about the ______ until they had already lost a lot of money.
4 ______ was abolished in the UK in 1969.
5 He's a social worker who helps ______ to adjust to life outside prison.
6 The murderer ______ for his crime.

# Crime

| | | |
|---|---|---|
| **to approach** | to go towards | sich nähern, zugehen auf |
| **to arrest** | to hold sb by law for committing a crime | festnehmen, verhaften |
| **bribery** | *v* to bribe | Bestechung |
| **decent** | respectable | anständig |
| **deputy** | the second person in a hierarchy | Hilfs-, Vertretung- |
| **to focus on** | to concentrate on sth | sich konzentrieren auf |
| **heavily-armed** | protected using weapons | schwer bewaffnet |
| **homicide** | murder | Tötung, Mord |
| **to impose** | to force | auferlegen, erlassen |
| **involvement** | being involved in sth | Beteiligung |
| **justice** | fair outcome | Gerechtigkeit |
| **liar** | *v* to lie | Lügner/in |
| **nationwide** | across the country | landesweit |
| **offence** | *n* offender | Delikt, Straftat |
| **policing** | *v* to police (an area) | Kontrolle, Überwachung |
| **policy** | e.g. government policy | Politik, Linie |
| **probation** | *phr* to put sb on probation | Bewährung |
| **to prosecute** | *n* prosecution | anklagen, strafrechtlich verfolgen |
| **puzzled** | confused | verdutzt |
| **to register** | to record | registrieren |
| **robbery** | *v* to rob | Raub, Überfall |
| **to speculate** | *n* speculation | spekulieren, Vermutungen anstellen |
| **speeding** | driving too fast | Geschwindigkeitsüberschreitung |
| **suspended sentence** | a possible punishment used as a threat | (Freiheits-)Strafe auf Bewährung |
| **tolerant** | able to endure/accept sth | tolerant |
| **turnaround** | big change | Kehrtwendung, Umschwung |
| **verdict** | e.g. a guilty verdict | Urteil, Beurteilung |
| **to weed out** | to get rid of | aussondern, -merzen |

## 1 Replace the underlined word with a word which means the same thing.

1 <u>Murder</u> is a federal offence.

______________________________

2 What was the <u>result</u> of the trial?

______________________________

3 He has committed several serious <u>crimes</u>.

______________________________

4 There was a dramatic <u>turnaround</u> in the city's crime figures.

______________________________

5 People everywhere are <u>wondering</u> about the verdict.

______________________________

## 2 Work out the anagrams.

1 I'm going to TECPORESU that young man for damaging my car!

______________________________

2 I think the government should work harder to DEWE OTU corrupt politicians.

______________________________

3 As it was his first offence, they put him on TROBPAOIN.

______________________________

4 The mayor's new YOPCIL on crime is very tough.

______________________________

5 The mafia is well-known for EBIRBYR.

______________________________

6 My new neighbours are all CEDNET people.

______________________________

7 Ms Barnacle is the new PUDEYT sheriff.

______________________________

8 He was arrested for SEGEPIDN on the first day after his driving test!

______________________________

# 12 Future life, future living

| | | |
|---|---|---|
| **abnormal** | <> normal | abnorm, ungewöhnlich |
| **to announce** | to declare | ankündigen |
| **astonishing** | *v* to astonish sb | erstaunlich |
| **ban** | *v* to ban sth | Verbot |
| **boycott** | refusing to buy or use a product | Boykott |
| **to be capable of** | to be able to | können, fähig sein |
| **cloning** | *v* to clone | Klonen |
| **conservation** | preservation, protection | Schutz, Erhaltung |
| **to diagnose** | *n* diagnosis | diagnostizieren |
| **doubt** | uncertainty | Zweifel |
| **exceptional** | unusually (positive) | außergewöhnlich |
| **genetically modified** | when genes have been altered in a food | genmanipuliert |
| **herd** | e.g. a herd of sheep | Herde |
| **hereditary** | *phr* a hereditary illness | erblich |
| **infection** | *adj* infectious | Entzündung |
| **ingredients** | one of the foods that make up a dish | Zutaten, Bestandteile |
| **to introduce** | to make sth available for use | einführen |
| **labelling** | *v* to label | Kennzeichnung |
| **loophole** | e.g. a legal loophole | Schlupfloch |
| **mammal** | e.g. cows, monkeys, whales | Säugetier |
| **miscarriage** | *v* to miscarry | Fehlgeburt |
| **offspring** | children | Nachkommen |
| **omission** | *v* to omit sth | Lücke |
| **premature** | unexpectedly early | vorzeitig, frühzeitig |
| **separate** | <> together | getrennt |
| **supporter** | *v* to support | Anhänger/in |
| **vast** | immense | riesig, ungeheuer |

## 1 Choose the sentence (a-c) which best describes the meaning of sentences 1 to 5.

1 He was born prematurely.

☐ a He was born early in the morning.
☐ b He was born too early.
☐ c He was very small when he was born.

2 Epilepsy is a hereditary illness.

☐ a You have a high chance of getting epilepsy if one of your parents has it.
☐ b Epilepsy is an illness that you can get by touching people with it.
☐ c Nobody knows how people get epilepsy.

3 Smoking is banned in most discos.

☐ a You can still smoke in most discos.
☐ b You are not allowed to smoke in most discos.
☐ c In most discos, people think that smoking is cool.

4 A loophole in the law means that supermarkets can sell unlabelled genetically-modified food.

☐ a The law clearly says that supermarkets have to label GM food.
☐ b It is the law that supermarkets have to label GM food.
☐ c A gap in the law means that supermarkets don't have to label GM food.

5 Scientists aren't yet capable of cloning humans.

☐ a Scientists still can't clone humans.
☐ b Scientists can clone humans already.
☐ c Scientists don't want to clone humans.

## 2 Replace the underlined words with suitable words or phrases from page 66.

1 The government <u>declared</u> that they would give money to three new research projects.

______________________________

2 The <u>protection</u> of our wildlife is very important to us.

______________________________

3 They invested <u>an immense</u> amount of money in the new project.

______________________________

4 There's a lot of <u>uncertainty</u> about whether the project will go ahead or not.

______________________________

# Future life, future living

| | | |
|---|---|---|
| **accidental** | unintentional | zufällig, versehentlich |
| **to alter** | to change | (ver)ändern |
| **breeding** | *v* to breed | Zucht, Züchtung |
| **by-product** | side effect, unintentional outcome | Nebenprodukt |
| **contrary** | *phr* on the contrary | Gegenteil |
| **consumption** | when sb uses/eats sth | Verzehr |
| **conventional** | traditional | konventionell, herkömmlich |
| **convincing** | persuasive | überzeugend |
| **downside** | disadvantage | Nachteil |
| **essential** | necessary | (unbedingt) notwendig |
| **flavour** | taste | Geschmack |
| **harmful** | *v* to harm sb/sth | schädlich |
| **to play havoc** | to ruin, to mess sth up | verheerende Schäden anrichten |
| **to imply** | *n* implication | andeuten, implizieren |
| **to interact** | to work with one another | sich gegenseitig beeinflussen |
| **to maintain** | to support | aufrechterhalten |
| **manipulation** | *v* to manipulate | Manipulation, Veränderung |
| **poisonous** | *n* poison | giftig |
| **potential** | possibilities | Potenzial |
| **predictable** | *v* to predict | voraussagbar |
| **shelf life** | date when a product expires | Haltbarkeit |
| **shortage** | not having enough of sth | Knappheit, Mangel |
| **to store** | to keep sth somewhere | lagern, aufbewahren |
| **substance** | matter | Substanz, Stoff |
| **tendency** | inclination, trend | Tendenz |
| **time-consuming** | requiring a lot of time | zeitraubend |
| **to trigger** | to make sth active | auslösen |
| **unintentional** | not on purpose | unabsichtlich |

## 1 Match the words to the definitions.

| | | | |
|---|---|---|---|
| 1 | breeding | a | what you think might happen |
| 2 | poisonous | b | harmful |
| 3 | flavour | c | producing young animals |
| 4 | manipulate | d | taste |
| 5 | prediction | e | influence something |

## 2 Match the sentences which have the same meaning.

1 It always takes ages in the post office.
2 He didn't mean to break the vase.
3 You need a work permit to get a job in Canada.
4 It was obvious she would go to university in London.
5 I thought she would go to Edinburgh, not London.

a It was unintentional.
b It's essential.
c It was contrary to what I thought.
d It was predictable.
e It's very time-consuming.

## 3 The underlined words are related to words in the list on page 68. Can you work out their German meanings?

1 They found no <u>alteration</u> – nothing had changed.

________________________________________

2 The scientist's research could <u>potentially</u> find a cure for AIDS.

________________________________________

3 It was an <u>accident</u>. I didn't mean to do it.

________________________________________

4 He couldn't <u>convince</u> me. I still think it's a bad idea.

________________________________________

5 I don't think it will do any <u>harm</u>. It's not that dangerous.

________________________________________

# 1 Internal combustion engines

| | | |
|---|---|---|
| **combustion chamber** | part of the engine where combustion takes place | Verbrennungskammer, Brennkammer |
| **component** | part, element | Komponente |
| **crank case** | part of the engine which encloses the crankshaft | Kurbelgehäuse |
| **cylinder head** | the part of the engine above the cylinders | Zylinderkopf |
| **durable** | long-lasting | widerstandsfähig |
| **dynamometer** | machine used to measure the amount of power generated by an engine | Kraftmesser |
| **environmentally-friendly** | not harmful to the environment | umweltfreundlich |
| **exhaust outlet** | where exhaust gases escape from an engine | Auslassöffnung |
| **frictional couple** | | Reibungskupplung |
| **intake** | e.g. fuel intake | Aufnahme, Einlass |
| **ignition** | *v* to ignite | Zündung |
| **intake outlet** | where air enters an engine | Einlass(öffnung) |
| **internal combustion engine** | engine where power is generated by an explosion | Verbrennungsmotor |
| **lubrication system** | system where oil ensures the smooth running of an engine | Schmiersystem |
| **to maintain** | to keep in good condition | warten, pflegen |
| **petrol** | a fuel for engines | Benzin |
| **piston** | a mechanical device that moves up and down | Kolben |
| **pressure** | force | Druck |
| **spark plug** | engine part which ignites fuel and starts engine | Zündkerze |
| **stroke** | a movement in an engine | Takt, Hub |
| **two-stroke engine** | a type of engine which functions using only two strokes of the piston | Zweitaktzyklus, Zweitaktverfahren |
| **valve** | a device which controls the flow of liquid/gas | Ventil |

## 1 Find the words which go together.

| | | | |
|---|---|---|---|
| 1 | frictional | a | plug |
| 2 | cylinder | b | case |
| 3 | exhaust | c | combustion |
| 4 | fuel | d | couple |
| 5 | crank | e | intake |
| 6 | spark | f | outlet |
| 7 | lubrication | g | head |
| 8 | internal | h | system |

## 2 Work out the anagrams to complete the sentences.

1 Most new car models are more OENMVYIRTALNLNE-RNLEFIDY than older ones.

______________________________

2 OWT-KROTSE GINSNEE are normally used to power portable equipment such as chainsaws.

______________________________

3 A YDENARMTMOE measures engine performance.

______________________________

4 Four-stroke engines use less LOPRET, so they are more fuel-efficient.

______________________________

5 If you AMINTNIA your engine well, it should work well for a long time.

______________________________

6 The third stroke in a four-stroke engine cycle is GNITINOI.

______________________________

7 The waste gases from an engine go out through the XHUEATS outlet.

______________________________

8 A LVAVE controls the direction of the petrol flow.

______________________________

9 An engine is made up of many different CMPOSNONET.

______________________________

10 The PESURERS in the cylinder head increases when the intake and exhaust outlets are closed.

______________________________

# 2 Electricity

| | | |
|---|---|---|
| **battery** | a cell which produces electric current | Batterie |
| **connecting wire** | a wire that joins two parts of a circuit | Verbindungskabel |
| **current** | *phr* electric current | Strom |
| **distribution** | *v* to distribute | Verteilung, Versorgung |
| **domestic housing** | private homes and houses | Privathaushalt(e) |
| **electric bell** | a bell powered by electricity | elektrische Klingel |
| **electric circuit** | path which electricity travels along | elektrischer Stromkreis, Schaltung |
| **electric motor** | motor powered by electricity | Elektromotor |
| **electric path** | a way or course through which electricity passes | elektrischer Pfad |
| **electric shock** | e.g. to get an electric shock | elektrischer Schlag |
| **to energize** | *n* energy | aufladen |
| **faulty** | broken | defekt |
| **to generate** | to create | erzeugen |
| **grid** | a system of electrical wires which distribute electricity | Stromnetz |
| **location** | *v* to locate | (Stand-)Ort |
| **power drill** | electric tool used to make holes | Elektrobohrer, Bohrmaschine |
| **power station** | power plant | Elektrizitätswerk, Kraftwerk |
| **pylon** | structure supporting wires above ground | Mast |
| **resistance** | opposition to the flow of a current | Widerstand |
| **switch** | device which turns sth on/off | Schalter |
| **tool** | device | Werkzeug, Instrument |
| **transformer station** | place where electric voltage is changed | Transformator, Umspannwerk |
| **to transmit** | to send an electronic signal | übertragen |
| **voltage** | a value used to measure electrical force | Spannung |

## 1 Find five words that you can combine with the word electric.

battery, bell, shock, circle, energy, circuit, path, motor, ring, surprise, dock, bath

## 2 Complete the puzzle to find the hidden word.

1 to send an electronic signal
2 to supply power to a machine
3 these are what you use to make or repair something
4 a system used to send electricity to other areas
5 buildings in which people live
6 something put inside another machine to produce electricity
7 this describes something which doesn't work properly
8 something made of metal which carries wires high above the ground
9 something used to turn an electric tool, light, etc. on or off
10 measurement of electrical force

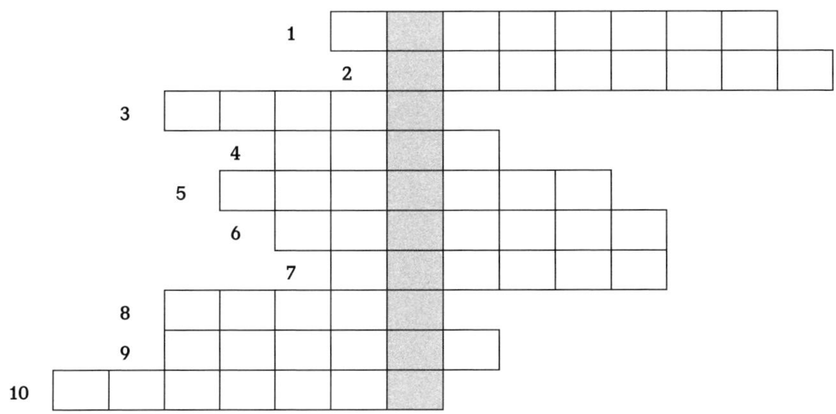

# Tools

| | | |
|---|---|---|
| **carpenter** | sb who works with wood | Zimmermann, Tischler/in |
| **chain saw** | power tool used to cut wood | Kettensäge |
| **chisel** | flat tool used to shape wood | Meißel |
| **circular saw** | a saw with a round metal disc wood, etc. | Kreissäge |
| **clockwise** | <> anticlockwise | im Uhrzeigersinn |
| **drill** | tool used to make holes | Bohrer |
| **electrician** | sb who connects and repairs electrical devices | Elektriker/in, Elektrotechniker/in |
| **to fix** | to repair | reparieren |
| **floorboard** | a piece of wood in a floor | (Holz-)Diele |
| **fretsaw** | saw used to cut patterns in wood, etc. | Laubsäge |
| **glue gun** | tool which melts glue | (Heiß)Klebepistole |
| **hacksaw** | tool used to cut metal | Bügelsäge |
| **hammer drill** | drill which makes holes using a quick pounding device | Bohrhammer |
| **to insert** | to put in, to add | einsetzen, -drehen |
| **to join** | to put together | verbinden, zusammenfügen |
| **lathe** | machine used to shape wood and metal | Drehbank, Drehmaschine |
| **mechanic** | sb who repairs engines | Mechaniker/in |
| **pipeline** | a tube which liquids and gases flow through | Rohr(leitung) |
| **power tool** | tool powered by a motor | Elektrowerkzeug |
| **to remove** | to take out | entfernen |
| **socket wrench** | tool used to tighten nuts/bolts | Steckschlüssel |
| **soldering iron** | tool which heats and joins wires | Lötkolben |
| **utility knife** | small knife with many different blades and tools | Universalmesser, Taschenmesser |
| **welder** | sb who joins pieces of metal together | Schweißer/in |
| **wheel** | e.g. car wheel | Rad, Reifen |

**1** **Put the words below in the correct category in the table. There are some words you don't need.**

soldering iron | hammer drill | floorboard | drill | chisel | wire | chain saw | hacksaw | wheel | lathe | glue gun | circular saw | socket wrench | pipeline | utility knife | fretsaw

| Power tool | Non-power tool |
|---|---|
| | |
| | |
| | |
| | |
| | |
| | |

**2** **Now find eight of the words above in the puzzle.**

| | | | | | | | | | | | | | |
|---|---|---|---|---|---|---|---|---|---|---|---|---|---|
| S | O | C | K | E | T | W | R | E | N | C | H | G | F |
| P | L | J | E | L | S | G | O | Y | Q | M | N | W | L |
| C | T | P | R | S | Y | X | V | K | L | I | P | K | O |
| I | M | I | W | R | Z | U | O | P | A | V | D | C | O |
| R | R | P | A | C | Y | W | I | R | E | U | R | S | R |
| C | L | E | D | H | W | I | P | A | E | L | I | M | B |
| U | Z | L | P | U | I | O | Z | T | R | E | L | A | O |
| L | A | I | S | W | H | E | E | L | D | F | L | G | A |
| A | H | N | J | Y | K | C | M | P | Y | D | G | K | R |
| R | H | E | L | A | T | E | W | S | F | J | Q | H | D |
| S | L | K | Z | E | R | X | B | N | M | I | P | C | B |
| A | M | B | C | A | D | G | J | L | O | U | W | S | J |
| W | X | N | H | T | A | E | W | B | P | S | X | L | P |
| P | S | O | L | D | E | R | I | N | G | I | R | O | N |
| L | A | Z | H | K | M | G | A | W | I | T | A | Q | L |

# 4 Materials and their properties

| | | |
|---|---|---|
| **alloy** | a mixture of two metals | Legierung |
| **cardboard** | e.g. cardboard box | Pappe |
| **conductor** | *v* to conduct | Leiter |
| **cotton** | a type of cloth | Baumwolle |
| **copper** | a type of metal | Kupfer |
| **durable** | strong, hard-wearing | langlebig |
| **fatal** | causing death | tödlich |
| **fragile** | easy to break or damage | zerbrechlich |
| **helmet** | e.g. bicycle helmet | Sturzhelm |
| **iron** | a type of metal | Eisen |
| **leather** | a material made from animal skin | Leder |
| **lead** | a type of metal | Blei |
| **malleable** | flexible | (ver)formbar |
| **to overtake** | to drive past the vehicle in front of you | überholen |
| **plastic** | a material produced by chemical processes | Plastik, Kunststoff |
| **to process** | to treat | verarbeiten |
| **rubber** | a substance made from the juice of tropical plants | Gummi |
| **to scratch** | to make a mark on a surface | kratzen |
| **shape** | form | Form |
| **shock-absorbing** | *v* to absorb | stoßdämpfend |
| **specification** | requirement | Vorgabe |
| **to speed** | to drive faster than is allowed | Geschwindigkeitsabgrenzung überschreiten |
| **state of the art** | modern, up-to-date | auf dem neusten Stand |
| **steel** | a type of metal | Stahl |
| **waterproof** | water-resistant | wasserdicht |
| **wood** | a material from trees | Holz |
| **wool** | a type of cloth | Wolle |

## 1 Read the definitions and decide which material it is.

1 This metal is used to build bridges and to make nails and tools.
2 Floorboards are often made of this. It comes from trees.
3 A natural material. Many clothes are made of this material.
4 This metal is brown and is used to cover 5, 2 and 1 cent coins.
5 This metal is not very environmentally-friendly and is poisonous for humans.
6 This is often used to make shoes.
7 A very warm material which comes mainly from sheep and is often used for clothing.
8 A man-made material. Many things around the house are made of this.
9 The symbol for this metal is Fe. It is the most commonly used of all metals.
10 This material comes from a tree and is used to make industrial gloves, for example.

## 2 Fill in the gaps with the correct words. There are two words you don't need.

speeding | state of the art | helmet | fragile | overtake | scratched | fatal

## POLICE REPORT

Local teenager Sam Lemont (16) was seriously hurt in an accident on Fourbridge Road, Harlow last Saturday at about 3 p.m. He was riding his bicycle towards Marylands Park when a man in a white Ford Escort van tried to ____________[1] him. The driver of the van was ____________[2] and didn't see the cyclist. Witnesses say he drove on towards the town centre, but that his van was badly ____________[3] when it hit the bicycle. The accident could have been ____________[4], but fortunately Mr Lemont was wearing a cycle ____________[5].

If you saw the accident or think you know the owner of the van, please contact Inspector Roberts on 0741 928437.

# 5 Energy

| | | |
|---|---|---|
| **access (to)** | *v* to access | Zugang (zu) |
| **alternately** | one after the other | abwechselnd |
| **apparatus** | equipment | Apparat, Gerät |
| **approximately** | about | ungefähr, etwa |
| **coal** | a fossil fuel | Kohle |
| **to compress** | <> to decompress | komprimieren |
| **concrete** | building material made from cement, sand and water | Beton |
| **considerable** | *v* to consider | beträchtlich, beachtlich |
| **to consist of** | to be made up of | bestehen aus |
| **consumption** | *v* to consume | Verbrauch |
| **core** | centre | Kern |
| **conservation** | *v* to conserve | Einsparung |
| **emission** | *v* to emit | Emission, Ausstoß |
| **energy source** | supply of energy | Energiequelle |
| **experiment** | test | Versuch, Experiment |
| **to flow into / out of** | to run into / out of | hineinfließen/abfließen |
| **geothermal** | connected to the internal heat of the earth | geothermal, mit Erdwärme |
| **hydropower** | power from water | Wasserkraft |
| **kinetic** | connected to motion | kinetisch |
| **nuclear fission** | releasing energy by splitting atoms | Kernspaltung |
| **renewable** | <> non-renewable | erneubar |
| **seabed** | the bottom of the sea/ocean | Meeresboden |
| **seawater** | water from the sea/ocean | Meerwasser |
| **solar energy** | energy from the sun | Sonnenenergie, Solarenergie |
| **sufficient** | enough | ausreichend, genugend |
| **surplus heat** | extra heat | überschüssige Wärme |
| **thermal** | connected with heat | thermisch |
| **tidal power** | energy from the sea | Gezeitenkraft |
| **uranium** | a radioactive element | Uran |

## 1 Match each kind of energy to its source.

| | | | |
|---|---|---|---|
| 1 | nuclear | a | seawater |
| 2 | hydroelectric | b | sun |
| 3 | tidal | c | earth's core |
| 4 | geothermal | d | water |
| 5 | solar | e | uranium |
| 6 | thermal | f | heat |

## 2 Replace the underlined words with one of the words or phrases below. There are two words you don't need.

access to · experiment · to consist of · solar · concrete · renewable · approximately · considerable · sufficient · consumption

1 There's <u>enough</u> petrol in the engine.

___

2 I need <u>to be able to get</u> the results of the experiments.

___

3 Our school building is made of <u>a mixture of cement, sand, stones and water</u>.

___

4 Oil <u>usage</u> is very high in industrialized countries.

___

5 Climate change may cause <u>very big</u> changes in the temperatures on earth.

___

6 The amount of energy produced from these two sources is <u>about</u> the same.

___

7 Wind energy is <u>a kind of energy which will not run out</u>.

___

8 We are doing a <u>test</u> to find out if this could be a 'green' source of energy in the future.

___

# 6 Safety

| | | |
|---|---|---|
| **biohazard** | a risk to health or the environment | biologische Gefährdung |
| **caution** | Be careful! | Vorsicht |
| **construction site** | building site | Baustelle |
| **corrosive** | *v* to corrode | ätzend |
| **cupboard** | closet | Schrank |
| **to damage** | to harm | schaden |
| **emergency** | a sudden dangerous event | Notfall |
| **escape route** | way out in an emergency | Fluchtweg |
| **to evacuate** | to leave | evakuieren, verlassen |
| **explosive** | *n* explosion | explosiv |
| **extension cable** | extra length of wire | Verlängerungskabel |
| **fire extinguisher** | device used to put out fires | Feuerlöscher |
| **flammable** | easily set on fire | (leicht) brennbar |
| **goggles** | protective glasses | Schutzbrille |
| **grinder** | a device that crushes sth | Schleifer |
| **hard hat** | helmet | Schutzhelm |
| **harness** | e.g. a safety harness | Gurt(e) |
| **harmful** | causing damage or injury | schädlich |
| **hazard** | risk, danger | Risiko, Gefahr |
| **injury** | *v* to injure | Verletzung |
| **to obstruct** | *n* obstruction | versperren, behindern |
| **protection** | *v* to protect | Schutz |
| **regulation** | rule | Bestimmung, Vorschrift |
| **scaffold** | structure workers use when constructing a building | (Bau-)Gerüst |
| **shelving** | shelves | Regal(e) |
| **toxic** | poisonous | giftig |
| **welding torch** | a tool used to join pieces of metal together | Schweißbrenner |
| **workshop** | an area where things are made and repaired | Werkstatt, Werkshalle |

**1** **Match the word parts below to make five safety hazards found on warning signs.**

| | | | | |
|---|---|---|---|---|
| BIO | OSIVE | CORR | FLAMM | HARM |
| HAZARD | OSIVE | FUL | EXPL | ABLE |

1 ______________________

2 ______________________

3 ______________________

4 ______________________

5 ______________________

**2** **Write the correct name of the object described in the sentences.**

1 This protects your head from falling objects: h______________________

2 These stop your eyes from getting burned: g______________________

3 A situation when people's lives might be in danger: e______________________

4 A closet where you can keep tools, chemicals, etc. c______________________

5 The place where builders work: c ______________________

6 A way to leave the building quickly (*2 words*): e______________________

7 You need to use one of these when something is burning (*2 words*): f______________________

8 This is useful if you need to take an electric tool far away from the wall (*2 words*):

e______________________

**3** **Find five things from in and around the workshop.**

weldingtorcharnesshelvinggogglescaffold

# 7 Supplying the global market

| | | |
|---|---|---|
| **amount** | quantity | Menge |
| **analysis** | *v* to analyze | Analyse |
| **assembly** | *v* to assemble | Zusammenbau, Montage |
| **barge** | a very large type of boat | Lastschiff, -kahn |
| **central depot** | main warehouse | Zentrallager |
| **containerization** | using containers | Verpackung in Container |
| **consumer** | person who buys goods or uses services | Verbraucher/in |
| **delivery** | distribution | (Aus-)Lieferung |
| **distribution** | *v* to distribute | Vertrieb, Lieferung |
| **filling station** | petrol station | Tankstelle |
| **fuel** | e.g. coal, diesel, oil, etc. | Treibstoff |
| **goods** | products | Waren, Güter |
| **haulage** | transport, forwarding | Spedition |
| **initial** | first | Anfangs- |
| **to load** | to put goods in a lorry, ship, etc. | laden |
| **offshore drilling rig** | where people drill for oil in the sea | Bohrinsel |
| **packaging** | e.g. can, bag, barrel, etc. | Verpackung |
| **palletization** | putting things on to pallets | Verteilung auf Paletten |
| **to pump** | to make water/air flow through a pipe | pumpen |
| **raw oil** | a type of fuel | Rohöl |
| **road tanker** | a lorry that transports oil, gas or petrol | Tanklastzug |
| **to schedule** | to plan, to set a timetable | einen Zeitplan aufstellen |
| **to ship** | to transport | versenden, verladen |
| **storage depot** | warehouse | Lagerhalle |
| **to supply** | to provide | beliefern |
| **supply chain** | production process from production to use | Versorgungskette |
| **warehousing** | storing of supplies | Lagerhaltung |

## 1 Sort the following words into the right category.

storage depot | container | pallet | ship | barge | warehouse | road tanker | fuel | raw oil

| Goods | Methods of storage | Methods of transport |
|---|---|---|
| | | |
| | | |
| | | |
| | | |

## 2 Work out the anagrams.

1 We need to find a more efficient way of delivering our products to our NOCMURESS.

2 It's important to HEDLUSEC deliveries very carefully.

3 We need to stop at a LIFNGIL TAOISTN to get more petrol.

4 Our company UMPPS gas through pipelines to certain areas of Western Europe.

5 The goods are DEDOLA onto delivery lorries outside the factory.

6 The TILNIIA planning of a project is the most important part.

7 Here is a diagram of the PSLUYP ACIHN: from production to delivery to the consumer.

8 She is an engineer and works on an ROSFOFHE LRIDLIGN GIR in the North Sea.

9 A private company makes the KPACGANGI for our products.

10 The goods are taken to the warehouse for storage and SALYSEMB.

# 8 Technical jobs

| | | |
|---|---|---|
| **ability** | skill | Fähigkeit |
| **to be based at** | to work in | seinen Sitz haben in |
| **client** | customer | Klient/in, Kunde/Kundin |
| **co-worker** | colleague | Kollege/Kollegin |
| **depending on** | according to | je nach |
| **to divide into** | to separate into | (unter)teilen |
| **employer** | *v* to employ | Arbeitgeber/in |
| **equipment** | tools, apparatus | Einrichtung, Gerät |
| **general duties** | tasks | allgemeine Aufgaben |
| **head office** | a company's main office | Hauptsitz, Zentrale |
| **heating technician** | a person who maintains heating systems | Heizungstechniker/in |
| **job advertisement** | *abbrev* job ad/advert | Stellenanzeige |
| **improvement** | *v* to improve | Verbesserung |
| **to install** | to set up | installieren |
| **IT specialist** | sb who works in IT | Fachinformatiker/in |
| **knowledge** | information, understanding | Wissen, Kenntnis |
| **to maintain** | to keep in good condition | warten, pflegen |
| **to meet deadlines** | to do something by an agreed time | Termine einhalten |
| **occupation** | job, profession | Beruf, Tätigkeit |
| **on own initiative** | without waiting for sb to tell you what to do | in Eigeninitative |
| **overtime** | *phr* to work overtime | Überstunden |
| **personal skills** | personal qualities | persönliche Fähigkeiten |
| **plumber** | sb who fits and repairs pipes, toilets, etc. | Installateur/in, Klempner/in |
| **to repair** | to fix | reparieren |
| **salary** | money you earn in a job | Gehalt |
| **technician** | sb who works with equipment and machinery | Techniker/in |
| **to train** | to teach | ausbilden, schulen |

**1** **Complete the letter with the correct translation of the German words.**

Dear Mr Morgan

I saw your ______________________________[1] (*Stellenanzeige*) in the Birmingham Reporter and would like to apply for the job of ______________________________[2] (*Heizungstechniker/in*) in your company.

I ______________________________[3] (*ausbilden, schulen*) for the job at Peterson Technics and I started working for my first ______________________________[4] (*Arbeitgeber*) soon after. My ______________________________[5] (*allgemeine Aufgaben*) were to ______________________________[6] (*installieren*) and ______________________________[7] (*pflegen*) all kinds of heating systems.

I think I would be good for the job because I have good ______________________________[8] (*persönliche Fähigkeiten*) and can work well in a team with my ______________________________[9] (*Kollegen*). Our company ______________________________[10] (*Kunden*) were always very happy with my work.

I am also able to work ______________________________[11] (*Überstunden*) when it is necessary to ______________________________[12] (*Termin einhalten*).

I enclose a copy of my CV.

Yours sincerely

Jocelyn Singh

# 9 Low-energy technology

| | | |
|---|---|---|
| **to achieve** | *n* achievement | erzielen |
| **advance** | progress | Fortschritt |
| **adviser** | *v* to advise | Berater/in |
| **boiler** | container which provides a building with hot water | Heißwasserspeicher; (Heiz-) Kessel |
| **cavity** | hollow space | Hohlraum |
| **combustion** | *v* to combust | Verbrennung |
| **to condense** | to become liquid | kondensieren |
| **configuration** | *v* to configure | Geräteanordnung |
| **cylinder thermostat** | a device which controls the temperate of a room | Zylinder Thermostat |
| **domestic** | connected with the home | häuslich |
| **double-glazing** | windows with two panes of glass to keep a room warm | Doppelverglasung |
| **exterior** | outside | äußere, Außen- |
| **efficient** | *n* efficiency | effizient, wirksam |
| **fan** | machine which creates a current of air | Ventilator |
| **ground-source** | geothermal energy | Erdwärme |
| **invisible configuration** | *v* to configure | unsichtbar Geräteanordnung |
| **mounted** | fixed or placed | befestigt |
| **photovoltaic cell** | solar cell which uses sunlight to create electricity | photoelektrische Zelle |
| **programmable** | *v* to programme | programmierbar |
| **radiator** | device which produces heat | Heizkörper |
| **to seal** | to close tightly | versiegeln |
| **steam engine** | a motor powered by steam | Dampfmaschine |
| **vapour** | steam | Dampf, Dunst |
| **visible** | <> invisible | sichtbar |
| **waste pipe** | a pipe which removes waste | Abflussrohr |
| **wind turbine** | a structure which produces energy from the wind | Windrad |

## 1 Complete the crossword.

1 a person who gives tips or helps with a problem

2 sth which gives you heat in a room

3 an empty space in a wall

4 a container in which water is heated to provide hot water or heating in a building

5 sth which works well and doesn't waste energy or money

6 private, at home

7 outside

8 a specially-shaped thermostat: ____________________ thermostat

## 2 Match the words which belong together.

| | | | |
|---|---|---|---|
| 1 | photovoltaic | a | pipe |
| 2 | steam | b | thermostat |
| 3 | waste | c | configuration |
| 4 | wind | d | glazing |
| 5 | double | e | cell |
| 6 | ground | f | turbine |
| 7 | invisible | g | engine |
| 8 | cylinder | h | source |

# 10 Easing the load

| | | |
|---|---|---|
| **air-tight** | not allowing air in or out | luftdicht |
| **arrangement** | *v* to arrange | Anordnung |
| **to calculate** | *n* calculation | berechnen |
| **to carry out** | to conduct | durchführen |
| **ceiling** | top of a room | (Zimmer-)Decke |
| **to demonstrate** | *n* demonstration | zeigen, demonstrieren |
| **to double** | to become twice as big | verdoppeln |
| **to exert** | *n* exertion | anwenden, ausüben |
| **factor** | aspect | Faktor |
| **formula** | e.g. a maths formula | Formel |
| **to halve** | *adj* half | halbieren |
| **hence** | therefore | daher |
| **leverage** | *v* to lever | Hebelwirkung |
| **mechanical advantage** | factor by which a mechanism increases the force exerted on it | Hebelübersetzung |
| **to multiply** | to increase | multiplizieren |
| **piston** | a mechanical device that moves up and down | Kolben |
| **principle** | concept | Prinzip |
| **pulley** | system using rope and wheels to lift heavy items | Rolle |
| **to reel in** | to wind in on a reel | einrollen, einholen |
| **shaft** | a metal bar which joins parts of a machine or engine | Achse, Welle |
| **significant** | considerable | erheblich |
| **tube** | a hollow pipe | Schlauch |

## 1 Complete the puzzle with the English terms to find the hidden word.

1 Faktor
2 luftdicht
3 durchführen
4 Achse
5 Decke
6 Hebelwirkung
7 anwenden
8 zeigen
9 Rolle
10 Prinzip
11 Schlauch

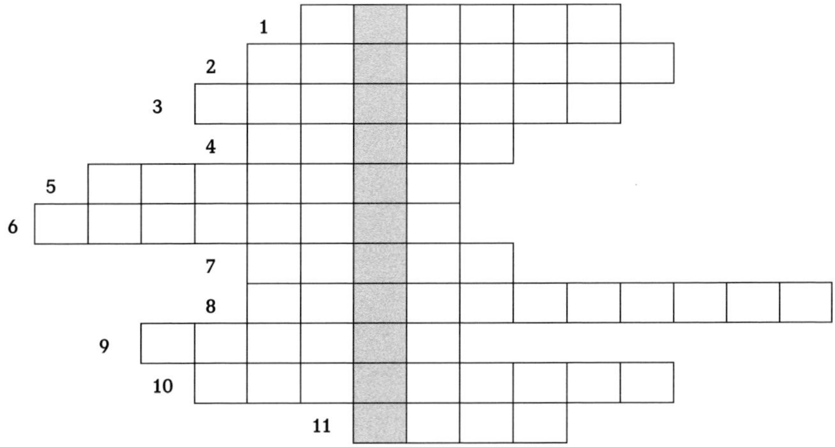

## 2 Find five words which you might use when talking about calculations.

| | | | | | | | | | |
|---|---|---|---|---|---|---|---|---|---|
| L | K | W | E | O | M | F | X | Q | M |
| H | A | L | V | E | P | O | Y | B | U |
| M | K | C | A | Z | B | R | A | H | L |
| A | D | F | H | C | L | M | N | Y | T |
| I | U | J | Y | D | B | U | L | E | I |
| X | A | V | P | O | C | L | W | I | P |
| C | A | L | C | U | L | A | T | E | L |
| P | L | M | I | B | J | R | N | U | Y |
| Z | G | E | V | L | E | S | Y | A | W |
| L | H | F | A | E | V | U | P | Y | S |

# 11 Data collection and storage

| | | |
|---|---|---|
| **abuse** | misuse | Missbrauch |
| **to alter** | *n* alteration | (ver)ändern |
| **backup** | a copy of a file | Sicherungskopie |
| **barrier** | sth that is in the way | Schranke, Barriere |
| **biometric** | using human features to identify people | biometrisch |
| **bitline** | | Bitleitung |
| **celebrity** | famous person | Prominente/r |
| **column** | vertical line | Spalte |
| **closed-circuit** | *phr* closed-circuit television (CCTV) | Überwachungs |
| **database** | set of data stored in a computer | Datenbank |
| **editor** | person in charge of a newspaper or magazine | Herausgeber/in |
| **to gather** | to collect | sammeln |
| **to intersect** | to cross | (sich) kreuzen |
| **leak** | giving away of secret information | undichte Stelle, Leck |
| **to monitor** | to keep a careful check on sth | überwachen, kontrollieren |
| **parliament** | people elected to rule a country | Parlament |
| **privacy** | *adj* private | Privatsphäre; Datenschutz |
| **risk** | danger, threat | Risiko |
| **row** | horizontal line | Zeile |
| **secure** | safe | sicher, geschützt |
| **to spy on** | to watch sb secretly | ausspionieren |
| **to store** | *n* storage | speichern |
| **theft** | crime of stealing sth | Diebstahl |
| **to track** | to follow | (zurück)verfolgen |
| **unmanned** | when a person is not needed to operate a machine | unbemannt |
| **wordline** | | Sprachleitung |

**1** **Decide which word is the odd one out and say why.**

1 gather – risk – store – leak

______________________________

2 celebrity – police officer – parliament – editor

______________________________

3 track – monitor – unmanned – spy on

______________________________

4 backup – abuse – murder – theft

______________________________

**2** **Find three pairs of synonyms and two pairs of opposites below. There are two words you don't need.**

wordline – electric – row – battery – intersect – alter – barrier – wall – column – bitline – change – cross

**Synonyms**

______________________________

______________________________

______________________________

**Opposites**

______________________________

______________________________

# 12 Robotics

| | | |
|---|---|---|
| **to adjust** | *n* adjustment | einstellen |
| **aerospace industries** | industry concerned with aeroplanes and space | Raumfahrtindustrie |
| **appearance** | look, form | Aussehen, Äußeres |
| **application** | *v* to apply | Anwendung |
| **axes** | *sing* axis | Achsen |
| **capacity** | *adj* capable | Kapazität, Leistung |
| **command** | order | Befehl |
| **construction** | *v* to construct | Konstruktion, Bauweise |
| **elbow rotation** | *v* to rotate | Ellbogenrotation |
| **feedback** | response | Rückmeldung |
| **forearm** | lower part of the arm | Unterarm |
| **humanoid** | human like | menschenähnlich |
| **industrial robot** | robot used in industry | Industrieroboter |
| **joint** | a place where two bones in the body join in a way which allows them to bend | Gelenk |
| **operation** | *v* to operate | Betrieb, Einsatz, Tätigkeit |
| **pitch** | part of a robotic arm | Neigung, Aufrichten |
| **precise** | exact | genau, präzise |
| **to programme** | to code, to instruct | programmieren |
| **robotics** | the science of robots | Robotertechnik |
| **roll** | part of a robotic arm | Rollen |
| **shoulder** | joint which attaches the arm to the body | Schulter |
| **sweep** | part of a robotic arm | Drehung, Schwenken |
| **swivel** | part of a robotic arm | Drehgelenk |
| **to transmit** | *n* transmission | übertragen |
| **wrist** | joint between the hand and the arm | Handgelenk |
| **yaw** | part of a robotic arm | Gieren |

## 1 Work out the anagrams.

1 I'm really interested in space so I would like to work in the AOERSEAPC ITNDSUYR.

______________________________

2 The robot was faulty – it didn't follow MOMASCND and do as it was told.

______________________________

3 The Japanese are very advanced in the field of OROBCTIS.

______________________________

4 They have developed a UHNAOMID robot to be a companion for old people.

______________________________

5 I need to JASDUT the settings so that it works properly.

______________________________

6 The main computer ARTSITNMS the data to the robot.

______________________________

## 2 Find five parts of a robotic arm in the grid.

| | | | | | | | | | |
|---|---|---|---|---|---|---|---|---|---|
| Y | R | H | Z | S | W | E | N | B | V |
| A | Y | A | W | J | I | U | T | C | H |
| S | F | R | T | R | O | L | L | F | R |
| J | E | E | P | M | T | Y | A | Z | S |
| S | J | K | P | S | E | W | P | M | W |
| A | T | L | I | G | S | D | B | N | I |
| Y | J | K | T | S | P | I | Y | E | V |
| C | U | P | C | S | D | Z | J | N | E |
| V | D | J | H | L | P | R | E | N | L |
| H | S | W | E | E | P | M | G | S | A |

# Answer key

**Refresher Course**

**Unit A**

**1** Neil has a part-time job in a clothes shop. 2 We usually go dancing in the city centre. 3 I like chilling out on the beach on holiday. 4 Kerstin and Danni are my best friends. 5 I spent a year doing voluntary work in India. It was hard but worthwhile. 6 Scientists haven't discovered a cure for cancer yet.

**Unit B**

**1** 1b; 2a; 3c; 4b

**2** opponent - teammate; tough - easy; disappointed - proud; nasty - nice; winner - loser; joke - Witz, Scherz; compete - konkurrieren

**Unit C**

**1** 1 cheeky; 2 get drunk; 3 weight; 4 refused; 5 sympathetic; 6 treatment; 7 attitude; 8 overcome

**2** 1 could no longer control; 2 embarrassed; 3 put on weight; 4 in no time

**Unit D**

**1** time up - time out; visum - visa; live expenses - living expenses; fly - flight; dark ideas - bright ideas; break out of - break into; come in - come on; school lefters - school leavers

**2** 1 proper; 2 watch out; 3 exciting/interesting destinations; 4 farewell; 5 give you a lift

**Unit E**

**1** 1 debts; 2 pushy; 3 touch; 4 repay; 5 features; 6 staff; 7 sale; 8 trolleys

**2** department store - the others are all people; irresponsible - the others are all positive ways of describing things/people; debt - the others are all words to do with saving money; credit - the others are all places where you can buy things

**Unit F**

**1** 1l; 2c; 3d; 4f; 5a; 6h; 7g; 8k

**2** 1 stay up; 2 complained about; 3 deal with

**3** 1C; 2B; 3A

## Main Course

### Unit 1A

1 ++ metropolis; + city; - town; - - village

2 opposite: calm - stressful, urban - rural, huge - tiny; same: downtown - city centre, yell - shout, amazing - impressive, non-stop - endless

3 1 cars; 2 wants to move back to the city; 3 non-stop; 4 endless; 5 believe

### Unit 1B

1 1 population; 2 immigration; 3 melting pot; 4 crowded; 5 explore; 6 draws; 7 variety; 8 under the sun; 9 breath; 10 man-made; 11 sense; 12 taxpayers

### Unit 2A

1 banner; classified; TV commercial; flyer; pop-up; poster; product placement; sponsorship

2 1 listed; 2 lance; 3 ship; 4 ment; 5 er

### Unit 2B

1 1a; 2b; 3c

2 1 decrease; 2 remain; 3 exaggerate; 4 fail; 5 gradual; 6 recover

### Unit 3A

1 1 running; 2 apologize; 3 celebrity; 4 audience; 5 latest; 6 background; 7 exploits; 8 launch; 9 clash; 10 viewers

### Unit 3B

1 1 stranger; 2 thief; 3 lazy; 4 honest; 5 rude; 6 at risk; 7 avoiding; 8 careful; 9 shout; 10 lied

2 1d; 2g; 3a; 4f; 5b; 6h; 7e; 8c

### Unit 4A

1 positive: delighted, pleased; negative: annoyed, frustrated, shocked, upset; neutral: amazed, surprised

2 1c; 2e; 3a; 4b; 5d

**Advertsing & media**

**1** Press: broadsheet, circulation, lead article, headline, supplement, tabloid; TV and film: box office hit, footage, plot, ratings, watershed

**2** 1 prime-time; 2 gap; 3 watershed; 4 licence; 5 sensationalist; 6 niche

**Unit 4B**

**1** 1b; 2b; 3b

**2** 1 benefit from; 2 congestion charging; 3 boot; 4 rush hour; 5 poor; 6 environmentally friendly; 7 electricity; 8 in common; 9 vehicle; 10 engine

**Unit 5A**

**1** 1 flood; 2 insulation; 3 progress; 4 reliable; 5 face; 6 turn down; 7 ran out; 8 epidemic; 9 brief; 10 average

**2** run out of: light bulbs, cash, milk, energy, ideas; turn down: an applicant, the heating, the music, an offer, the oven; get rid of: an old sweater, light bulbs, a headache, a problem, debts, the evidence

**Unit 5B**

**1** 1 act, stop; 2 warning; 3 Thanks to; 4 amount; 5 Very bad

**2** impossible - possible; safety - danger; rare - common; freeze - melt; extra words: global, nuclear

**Transport & environment**

**1** 1h; 2a; 3c; 4f; 5b; 6d; 7g; 8e

**2** 1 insufficient; 2 felled; 3 wildlife; 4 reforestation; 5 dump; 6 lane: 7 runway

**Unit 6A**

**1** 1 deal with; 2 temporary; 3 receptionist; 4 vocational; 5 varied; 6 travel agent; 7 instructor; 8 salary; hidden job: waitress

**2** 1 employer - others are words which describe a job; 2 company benefits - others are all explicitly about money; 3 flight attendant - all the others work in an office; 4 secretary - all the others are companies/employers

### Unit 6B

**1** 1b; 2e; 3a; 4f; 5c; 6d

**2** 1 employee; 2 cafeteria; 3 develop; 4 commitment; 5 invest

**3** 1 workforce; 2 generosity; 3 cafeteria; 4 terms, contract; 5 subsidized

### Unit 7A

**1** 1 paycheck; 2 done overtime; 3 a cutting-edge; 4 ordered; 5 an opportunity; 6 felt uncomfortable; 7 they shook hands; 8 pleasant, amusing; 9 made an excuse; 10 rarely saw; 11 explanation

### Unit 7B

**1** 1 relies; 2 examining; 3 middlemen; 4 strengths, weaknesses; 5 shareholders

**2** 1 target; 2 casual; 3 widely; 4 middlemen; 5 picker; 6 bury

### Unit 8A

**1** 1d; 2c; 3b; 4f; 5a; 6e

**2** 1 duties; 2 sectors; 3 referees; 4 accommodation; 5 abilities; 6 expenses

### Unit 8B

**1** 1b; 2a; 3a; 4b; 5a

**2** 1 korrupt; 2 Rat; 3 auswandern; 4 bürokratisch; 5 irreführen

### Work & globalization

**1** 1b; 2a; 3c; 4b

**2** 1 domestic; 2 apprentice; 3 insource; 4 promotion; 5 import; 6 sweatshop

### Unit 9A

**1** 1c; 2d; 3b; 4a; 5e; 6f

**2** 1 rejected; 2 abandoned; 3 childminder; 4 customs; 5 cared for; 6 musician; 7 retirement; 8 addiction; 9 social services

### Unit 9B

1 1 suffragette; 2 (protest) marches; 3 arrested; 4 population; 5 disobedience; 6 united; 7 achieve; 8 powerful; 9 battle; 10 concerned with

### Unit 10A

1 1b; 2d; 3e; 4c; 5f; 6a

2 1 rowdy; 2 monotonous; 3 perplexed; 4 trembling; 5 demanded; 6 setting; 7 countless; 8 forbidden

### Unit 10B

1 1 census; 2 uniform; 3 multiracial; 4 deport; 5 reflects; 6 intermarriage; hidden word - respondent

2 1 willing, out-dated; 2 respondents; 3 tremendous, appeal; 4 applies; 5 shrank; 6 enable, unclear

### Unit 11A

1 1 punishment; 2 ransom; 3 clemency; 4 remorse; 5 victim; 6 burglary; 7 murder; 8 attempt

2 1b; 2e; 3a; 4f; 5c; 6d

3 1 victims of crime; 2 ransom money; 3 bank fraud; 4 capital punishment; 5 reformed criminals; 6 showed remorse

### Unit 11B

1 1 homicide; 2 verdict; 3 offences; 4 change; 5 speculating

2 1 prosecute; 2 weed out; 3 probation; 4 policy; 5 bribery; 6 decent; 7 deputy, 8 speeding

### Unit 12A

1 1b; 2a; 3b; 4c; 5a

2 1 announced; 2 conservation; 3 a vast; 4 doubt

### Unit 12B

1 1c; 2b; 3d; 4e; 5a

2 1e; 2a; 3b; 4d; 5c

3 1 Änderung; 2 potenziell; 3 Zufall; 4 überzeugen; 5 Schaden

## Technical Topics

### Technical Topic 1

**1** 1d; 2g; 3f; 4e; 5b; 6a; 7h; 8c

**2** 1 environmentally-friendly; 2 two-stroke engines; 3 dynamometer ; 4 petrol; 5 maintain; 6 ignition; 7 exhaust; 8 valve; 9 components; 10 pressure

### Technical Topic 2

**1** bell, circuit, motor, path, shock

**2** 1 transmit; 2 energize; 3 tools; 4 grid; 5 housing; 6 battery; 7 faulty; 8 pylon; 9 switch; 10 voltage; hidden word - resistance

### Technical Topic 3

**1** power tools: chain saw, circular saw, fretsaw, hammer drill, lathe, glue gun, soldering iron; non-power tools: chisel, drill, hacksaw, socket wrench, utility knife; words not used: floorboard, pipeline, wheel, wire

**2** wire, drill, pipeline, soldering iron, socket wrench, wheel, circular saw, floorboard

### Technical Topic 4

**1** 1 steel; 2 wood; 3 cotton; 4 copper; 5 lead; 6 leather; 7 wool; 8 plastic; 9 iron; 10 rubber

**2** 1 overtake; 2 speeding; 3 scratched; 4 fatal; 5 helmet

### Technical Topic 5

**1** 1e; 2d; 3a; 4c; 5b; 6f

**2** 1 sufficient; 2 access to; 3 concrete; 4 consumption; 5 considerable; 6 approximately; 7 renewable; 8 experiment

### Technical Topic 6

**1** biohazard, corrosive, explosive, flammable, harmful

**2** 1 hard hat; 2 goggles; 3 emergency; 4 cupboard; 5 construction site; 6 escape route; 7 fire extinguisher; 8 extension cable

**3** welding torch, harness, shelving, goggles, scaffold

### Technical Topic 7

**1** goods: fuel, raw oil; methods of storage: container, storage depot, pallet, warehouse; methods of transport: barge, road tanker, ship

**2** 1 consumers; 2 schedule; 3 filling station; 4 pumps; 5 loaded; 6 initial; 7 supply chain; 8 offshore drilling rig; 9 packaging; 10 assembly

### Technical Topic 8

**1** 1 job advertisement; 2 heating technician; 3 trained; 4 employer; 5 general duties; 6 install; 7 maintain; 8 personal skills; 9 co-workers/colleagues; 10 clients; 11 overtime; 12 meet deadlines

### Technical Topic 9

**1** 1 adviser; 2 radiator; 3 cavity; 4 boiler; 5 efficient; 6 domestic; 7 exterior; 8 cylinder

**2** 1e; 2g; 3a; 4f; 5d; 6h; 7c; 8b

### Technical Topic 10

**1** 1 factor; 2 air-tight; 3 carry out; 4 shaft; 5 ceiling; 6 leverage; 7 exert; 8 demonstrate; 9 pulley; 10 principle; 11 tube; hidden word - arrangement

**2** calculate, double, formula, halve, multiply

### Technical Topic 11

**1** 1 risk: all the other words describe ways of dealing with information; 2 parliament: all the other words describe one person; 3 unmanned: all the other words describe ways of watching a person; 4 backup: all the other words describe crimes

**2** synonyms: alter - change, barrier - wall, cross - intersect; opposites: bitline - wordline, column - row

### Technical Topic 12

**1** 1 aerospace industry; 2 commands; 3 robotics; 4 humanoid; 5 adjust; 6 transmits

**2** pitch, roll, sweep, swivel, yaw